Songs in the Garden

Songs in the Garden

Poetry in the Gardens of Ancient Japan

Marc Peter Keane

The color paintings of *yanagi* on the front cover and
asagao on the back cover are by the author.
The monochrome paintings throughout the book are also
by the author and the calligraphy on them is Kyoko Selden's hand.

Contents

Acknowledgments

First and foremost, I would like to thank Kyoko Selden, researcher, writer and translator of Japanese, who worked with me on this book, guiding my unsteady attempts at translating the poems, and sharing with me her extensive knowledge of classical Japanese literature and culture. It is no understatement to say that I couldn't have done it without her. So much of what I have come to understand about Heian-period poetry is due entirely Kyoko's generosity with her time and knowledge. As if that were not enough, the beautiful calligraphy that overlays my paintings throughout the book was also painted by Kyoko.

I first came across the idea of a link between poetry and gardens in Japan in Wybe Kuitert's book, *Themes, Scenes, and Taste in the History of Japanese Garden Art*. The image he presented of *yamabuki* flowers reflecting in water stayed with me. After working on the translation of the Heian-period gardening treatise, *Sakuteiki*, with Professor Jirō Takei, I felt one thing missing in that ancient treatise was the relationship of poetry and gardens — so important at that time — and that led to the writing of this book.

I would like to mention two sources of information that made the research for this book both expedient and pleasurable. The first is the Carl A. Kroch Library at Cornell University, where I am a visiting fellow in the East Asia Program. I would especially like to thank Daniel McKee, Japanese bibliographer, who kindly helped me navigate the seemingly limitless resources available through the library. Secondly, a word of thanks to the Japanese Text Initiative, a collaborative effort between the University of Virginia Library Electronic Text Center and the University of Pittsburgh East Asian Library to make texts of classical Japanese literature available on the World Wide Web, and the like-named Japanese Historical Text Initiaitive of the University of California, Berkeley. The ease with which classical poetry texts and other historical documents can be accessed and searched using their systems was exceptional.

I would also like to thank Beth Cary, editor and translator/interpreter of Japanese, for her excellent and careful review of my manuscript. Her gleaning of errata, comments on style and consistency, and insights into many aspects of the text made this a better book.

ASAGAO

kienu ma no

mi wo wa shirushiru

asagao no

tsuyu to arasou

yo wo nageku kana

Murasaki Shikibu Shū 53

MORNING GLORY

I know it all so well

we're here   then we're gone

condemned to race

the fleeting dew   the fading flower

what a sad, sad world this is

きえぬ香の　身とはしりつゝ

朝顔の　露とや

夜を驚かす

It is summer in Japan, sometime in the early 11th century. Even in the early morning, the heat is oppressive, waking the cicadas to begin their constant whirring. In the northeast quarter of the imperial capital, Heian-kyō, lies a residence that has fallen into disrepair through the vicissitudes of time, the main house a mere shadow of its former self. The garden, however, has recently been refurbished and looks enchanting. Genji, the Shining Prince, second son of Emperor Kiritsubo, sits inside, visiting his true love, Murasaki no Ue, who is very ill, tormented by the possessing spirit of the deceased Rokujō Lady. Murasaki's floor-length black hair, newly washed and shining, flows about her where she lies. She appears to Genji particularly beautiful despite her tenuous state. Or, perhaps, because of it.

From the room where Genji attends Murasaki, he can see the pond in the garden through the fine bamboo blinds that hang in front of the veranda. Lotuses grow thickly in the water, lifting their broad leaves and exquisite flowers up above the surface toward the sky. The scene appears wonderfully cool on that hot summer day. Genji, in an attempt to lift Murasaki's spirits, points out the little drops of dew that shine like jewels on the lotus leaves. She sits up to look, ghost-like, her pale skin as transparent as the discarded husk of a cicada. Watching her with tears in his eyes, Genji tells her that he, too, has felt that at any moment he might slip away into that other world that awaits. She responds with a poem.

消えとまる　ほどやは経べき　たまさかに　はちすの露の　かかる許を

kie tomaru　hodo ya wa fubeki　tamasaka ni　hachisu no tsuyu no　kakaru bakari wo

Could it be
    I will disappear, having lasted
       not much longer
Than the pearls of dew
      that barely cling to the lotus leaves

Genji replies,

契おかむ　この世ならでも　はちす葉に　玉ゐる露の　心へだつな

chigiri okamu　kono yo narademo　hachisuba ni　tama iru tsuyu no　kokoro hedatsu na

Let us promise
    that not just in this life
      our hearts will be as one
As close as jeweled drops of dew
    beaded on a lotus leaf[1]

They gaze out at the garden and poems flow from their lips.

Therein lies the gist of this book. That in the Heian period (794–1185), the imagery of poems, known only too well by the imperial courtiers, and the imagery of the gardens they built at their residences were so completely intertwined and interrelated, that when a garden was observed it was understood by the viewer in a poetic manner. Not simply as an object to be appreciated visually, a lovely thing like a picture or a sculpture, well-designed and balanced with its various colors and textures properly arranged, but something that was filled with symbolic imagery, visual metaphors derived from a well-known body of poetry.

The idea of looking at a natural scene and immediately imagining a poem was given expression by the compilers of the *Kokin Wakashū*, an imperial anthology of poems completed by the early years of the 10th century. The *Kokin Wakashū*, or *Kokinshū* as it is commonly referred to, was one of the most widely read anthologies available to the Heian-period courtiers. One of its compilers, Ki no Tsurayuki, began the preface to the anthology with these lines.

The poetry of Yamato (old Japan) is like a seed in the heart of our people, which has unfurled as myriad-leaved songs. All the events of people's lives — the things they see and hear, and what they hold in their hearts — come forth as poems. He who hears a bush warbler chirping amid the flowers or a frog crying from its watery home, who could live among such living things and not want to write a poem?[2]

When Tsurayuki describes the overwhelming desire to compose a poem, it is in reaction to certain scenes of wild nature. Many of the elements of poetic inspiration that were to be found in the wild, however, were also to be found in the gardens of Heian-period courtiers. This happened either by design, such as was the case with pine trees, water reeds, or streams, just to mention three elements that were poetic motifs and also purposefully designed into the gardens. Or it happened by chance as in the case of the bush warbler and frog mentioned above, or moonlight and mist, all of which were poetic motifs that could be, and were, seen in gardens even though they were not intentionally put there.

Thus, for the courtiers, looking at a garden, like looking at wild nature, would immediately bring to mind numerous poetic references and images.

The garden was no longer an inert object. Through the medium of poetic imagery the garden was given new levels of meaning and mediums of expression. It was as if the garden had been given a voice and, waxing unabashedly romantic here, with that voice could sing. I say sing, because poems at that time were often "sung," or perhaps "chanted" evokes the correct image. In fact, the line that separated poetry and song was so indistinct that one word, *uta*, was used for both meanings. What follows in this book is the story of how poetry and gardens were connected or, put another way, the story of the songs in the garden.

Life in the Heian Capital

The previously mentioned scene between Prince Genji and Murasaki comes from *Genji Monogatari, The Tale of Genji*, the early-11th-century novel that follows the loves and losses of one Prince Genji, son to the emperor of Japan. In telling Genji's personal tale, the story also captures the lifestyles of the imperial courtiers in the Heian era: details such as their daily habits, superstitions, clothes, residences, gardens, poetry, and much more. From this story, as well as information from other literary, painterly, and archeological sources, we can get a good sense of what their lives were like.

Although some courtiers were stationed in far-flung provinces, most lived in a city called Heian-kyō, the Capital of Tranquility and Peace, often referred to simply as Heian. The city gives name to the era, the Heian period, which began with the founding of the city in 794 and ended nearly four hundred years later, when the new military government set up its capital in distant Kamakura in 1185. Heian-kyō was a city of perhaps 100,000 inhabitants, which made it one of the largest cities in the world at that time. Yet of that total population only an estimated ten percent or less belonged to the courtier class. This class included the imperial family, high-ranking families, such as the Fujiwara, who supported the imperial family and their government (and, in the case of the Fujiwara, eventually wrested control of the government for themselves), and also included the many lower-ranking men and women who waited at court, staffed the government offices, and carried out the activities of the government.

The design of the Heian capital was based on that of another city,

Chang'an (modern-day Xian), the imperial capital of Tang-dynasty China. Accordingly, Heian, like Chang'an, was geometrically formal in its layout, a rectangle in its overall shape, about 5.2 km (3.2 miles) north to south and 4.5 km (2.8 miles) east to west. The city was subdivided into a grid pattern of blocks by a series of broad avenues, minor streets, and narrow alleyways. The imperial palace and halls of state were located within a large, walled compound that lay along the center of the northern edge of the city. From the southern gate of that compound, a broad avenue named Suzaku-ōji ran south through the middle of the city, splitting it into east and west halves that were intended to be mirror images of each other. In practice, however, things were not so equal. Because the natural environmental conditions were better in the northeastern portion of the city, with plenty of available fresh water but without the accompanying swampy land found in the southwest, it was in the northeast that the courtiers of highest standing kept their residences. To a great degree, the gardens described in this book were to be found on the grounds of those homes.

Within this very formally structured city, the courtiers lived formally structured lives as part of a highly developed system of court culture. A perfect example of how the imperial bureaucracy reflected the physical arrangement of the city was the designation of various Offices of the Left and Right in which ministers were assigned symmetrical positions even as the city was split in identical halves. In many other ways, too, the courtiers' lives were dictated by the framework of court society. There were, for instance, many annual ceremonies they took part in, several every month in fact. Early spring would find them gathering the plants for the Festival of Seven Herbs, *nanakusa no sekku*,[3] at which seven medicinal herbs were collected and used to flavor rice porridge. There was the summertime purification ceremony, *tango no sechie*,[4] when medicinal plants such as sweet rush and mugwort were used to cleanse their homes of evil spirits. And in one of the autumn harvest festivals called *toyo no akari no sechie*,[5] the emperor ceremonially partook of newly harvested rice to bless the bounty of the lands.

The aspect of Heian courtiers' lives that is most important to this book, however, is their education — formal and informal. Both men and women of the courtier class were expected to be educated in the culture of their society, but their education differed. In short, men were taught in formal settings, while women studied informally at home. Men were required to study classical Chinese texts whether at the Imperial University or at private institutions supported by various families. These would have included Chinese classics focused on Confucianist thought such as the *Analects* (pinyin, *Lun Yu*; Japanese, *Rongo*; 論語), which are purportedly the records of the philosopher Confucius and his disciples, and *The Classic of Filial Piety* (pinyin, *Xiaojing*; Japanese, *Kōgyō*; 孝経), a text that gives advice on proper social order. Others classics helped with learning to read and write Chinese such as *The Thousand Character Classic* (pinyin, *Qianziwen*; Japanese, *Senjimon*; 千字文), a Chinese poem that was used as a primer for teaching Chinese characters to beginners. Still other texts introduced the concepts of geomancy, the Chinese physics that guided so many decisions in Heian-period lives. These included the *Classic of Changes* (pinyin, *Yijing*; Japanese *Ekikyō*; 易 經), one of the oldest of the classic texts that describes the divination system, and *The Five Phase Compendium* (pinyin, *Wuxing Dayi*; Japanese, *Gogyō Taigi*; 五行大義) that focused on another aspect of geomancy. In addition, they would have studied poetry. There were collections of works by Chinese poets (compiled by both Chinese and Japanese editors) as well as anthologies of Japanese poems. Women were not taught in formal university settings, and they were not typically schooled in Chinese letters, but they did learn poetry, and it is this last aspect of Heian-period courtier society — that both men and women were well-versed in poetry — that is so important to this story.

Poetry in Heian Life

The education from childhood of a person associated with the Heian court, formal or otherwise, would have necessarily included the study of poetry. Some of those poems were Chinese and would have been studied through compendiums of classical Chinese or Chinese-style poetry, *kanshi* (漢詩), which included the following: *Kaifūsō* (懐風藻), the oldest compendium of *kanshi* written by Japanese poets completed in 751; *Bunka Shūreishū* (文華秀麗集), and *Wakan Rōeishū* (和漢朗詠集), which included both Japanese and Chinese poetry.

Other poems were Japanese in origin and existed in imperial anthologies such as the *Kokinshū* and the older anthology, the *Man'yōshū*. Poetry influenced many aspects of social interaction among the courtiers, from a simple letter of thanks written after a visit, to a formal state gathering. Poetry contests were featured in court life. Courtiers and court ladies could make their mark on court society, or lose face, based on their ability to compose poems on the spot.

One such contest is mentioned in the beginning of the Hana no en chapter of *Genji Monogatari*. In this case, gentlemen courtiers gathered in the large open courtyard in front of the main ceremonial hall. They were called forward one by one in order of rank to be granted a Chinese character, at which time they would call out loudly the name of the character they received. In the Hana no en chapter, for instance, Prince Genji receives the character meaning spring. The contestants used the character they received to construct a rhyming poem in the Chinese mode of composition, *kanshi*. This process of receiving characters to make rhymes was referred to as *tan'in*, "searching for rhymes."[6]

If the scenes captured in Heian-period literature are to be taken as fact, then courtiers also engaged in poetic repartee verbally, as well as in writing, which would have required an even greater affinity with the material to be able to compose at a moment's notice. Take, for instance, the aforementioned scene between Genji and Murasaki. They look at lotuses in the garden and create impromptu poems as naturally as if they were simply chatting with each other. And this is not the only time this happens in *Genji Monogatari*. Time and time again, one or another of the characters in the story will be resting on the veranda, gazing out at the garden in a state of languor or passion, and some aspect of the garden will trigger a thought or a memory which comes flowing out, full-born as a poem. The poem might be a derivation of an existing poem, drawn from one of the classical anthologies of poems, or it may be something new and spontaneous. The themes of the impromptu poems that appear in *Genji Monogatari* were various: bluebells, snow, yellow-rose bushes, bamboo, smoke from firelights, a warbler on a plum tree, bush clover, cuckoo birds, and red plum blossoms scattering petals and perfume. In each instance, just the sight or sound of the thing was enough to inspire the viewer to create a poem. Here are a few other examples from *Genji Monogatari*, to give a sense of how these poems appear in the story.

The first example revolves around snow and ice in the garden. Genji enjoys nothing better than a conquest — in love not war. His pursuit of court ladies forms the core of the story. Princess Asagao, the Shrine Priestess, however, has always rebuffed his approaches. In the Asagao chapter he attempts to woo her again and is rejected once more, leaving him distraught as he returns home. The night is cold — snow blankets the garden, ice covers the pond. Genji has the screens along the veranda rolled up so that he can see the moonlight on the garden as he sits with Murasaki, his adopted daughter turned lover, and talks about the various women he has known. She sings a poem to him, using the image of the frozen water in the garden to evoke her own inner feelings and that of the moon to represent Genji.

こほりとぢ　石間の水は　ゆきなやみ　空すむ月の　かげぞながるる
koori toji ishima no mizu wa yuki nayami sora sumu tsuki no kagezonagaruru

> Frozen solid
>> the stream's water locks onto the stones
>>> finding no way to go
> Only the luminous moonlight
>> flows easily through the clear sky[7]

Genji looks at her and, finds her more beautiful than ever — the way her long hair falls, the quality of her face. In the garden, Mandarin ducks cry their mournful songs. Known as *oshi* or *oshi-dori*, Mandarin ducks purportedly mate for life and, consequently, are a symbol in China and Japan of life-long fidelity. Hearing their cries, Genji is moved to make an expression of faithful love to Murasaki, to whom he has been anything but faithful. He returns with:

かきつめて　むかし恋しき　雪もよに　あはれをそふる　をしのうきねか
kakitsumete mukashi koishiki yuki moyoni aware wo souru oshi no ukine ka

> All those memories
>> of good times now past　　gather
>>> like this endless falling snow
> Joined in sweet sadness
>> two Mandarin ducks　　asleep on the waters

The next example from *Genji Monogatari* of poetry composed on the spot about something seen in the garden comes from the Kochō chapter.

Genji is pursuing a young girl, Tamakazura, courting her in her residence and, as he leaves, notices a patch of Chinese bamboo, *kuretake*, growing in the garden. Genji is pleased by the sight of the young supple plant (reflecting his desire for a young pliant lover), and stops to contemplate it. He offers:

ませのうちに　根ふくうへし　竹の子の　おのが世々にや　生ひわかるべき
mase no uchi ni　nefukaku uweshi　take no ko no　ono ga yoyo ni ya　oiwakarubeki

> The young bamboo shoot
>> whose roots I planted so well and deep
>>> protected within my garden fence
> Has the time come for it to leave
>> to live its own life out in the world[8]

She responds,

今さらに　いかならむ世か　若竹の　生いはじめけむ　根をばたづねん
imasara ni　ikanaramu yo ka　wakatake no　oihajimekemu　ne wo ba tazunen

> After all this
>> would the time ever come
>>> for this young bamboo
> To search out the root
>> from which it first sprang[9]

One last example, though there are many others, comes from the Yadorigi chapter. The Emperor is scheming to have Kaoru, the purported son of Genji (but, in fact, not his true offspring), marry his daughter, Onna Ni no Miya. He invites the young man to the palace and they play some rounds of the board game called *go*, the Emperor intimating that he has something of great value at stake. When they are done and the Emperor has lost (on purpose, perhaps), he tells Kaoru that he will let him pluck a flower from the garden. Kaoru, taking the hint, goes down into the garden and picks a chrysanthemum bloom. When he returns indoors he sings in a serious tone:

世のつねの　垣根ににほふ　花ならば　こころのままに　おりて見ましを
yo no tsune no　kakine ni nihou　hana naraba　kokoro no mama ni　orite mimashi wo

> If it were just a flower
>> blooming brightly in the kind of hedge
>>> one sees so commonly
> I would have reached out and plucked it
>> to my heart's satisfaction[10]

The Emperor replies:

霜にあへず　枯れにし園の　菊なれど　残りの色は　あせずもある哉
shimo ni aezu　karenishi sono no　kiku naredo　nokori no iro wa　asezu mo arukana

> Here it lies withered
>> a garden defeated by the frost
>>> yet look　　　this chrysanthemum
> The color that remains
>> hasn't faded a bit[11]

Time and time again, we find this happening. People see something in the garden — a plant in bloom, a bird, ice or snow, withered grasses — and they find that an old poem from one of the imperial anthologies is brought to mind, or, as likely as not, they are inspired to compose a new poem on the spot. For the Heian courtiers, the garden was not only beautiful, it was a reminder and a well-spring of poetic thoughts.

Surely not all courtiers, however, were drop-dead talented poets. Probably far from it. There are interesting references in the diaries of the time that talk derisively about people who make pretenses to being poets when they are not. In one of the most famous of those diaries, *Makura no Sōshi*, *The Pillow Book*, the author, Sei Shōnagon, who was an upper-level lady-in-waiting, captures an interesting scene at court that touches on this. The Emperor and Empress are attended in a room by a number of their ladies-in-waiting. The Emperor commands that Shōnagon grind some ink on an inkstone and folds up a piece of paper, asking each person in attendance to quickly write down the first ancient poem they can think of. It is a test, of course, to see which of the ladies has any knowledge of poetry. The Empress then jumps in, producing a copy of the *Kokinshū*, which she begins to read. She calls out the first part of a poem, and asks for those attending to supply the second portion. Unfortunately, they all do very poorly, able only to give five or ten answers each when in fact the *Kokinshū* holds over a thousand poems. The Empress scolds them for not copying out the *Kokinshū*, saying that if they had done this several times, they would have been able to complete all the poems she read. She goes on to relate the story of a lady-in-waiting at the time of Emperor Murakami who had memorized every last poem in the *Kokinshū*.[12]

Two interesting points are made here. The first is that the *ideal* among the courtiers was to have a perfect knowledge of poetry, to be well-read in the anthologies and to be quick enough of wit to be able to recite a classical poem, or a modified rendition of one, on the spot. The other point made is that, although that ideal was accepted by the courtiers, the *reality* was that it was only actually attained by a few. I am not trying to create or sustain an illusion that the people of the Heian-period court were gossamer creatures who floated about spouting poems to each other all day. Naturally, they were not. The individuals of their society attained the ideals of their society perhaps no more than people do today. There were probably some courtiers who preferred riding horses and hunting to composing poems, and others who wanted with all their hearts to be light with words but, unfortunately, were desperately tongue-tied despite their wishes. Still, skill at poetry was a paradigm they aspired to, and knowledge of poetry was a very real requirement of their society. If nothing else, poetry was their first and foremost form of entertainment and, as such, it was as central to their thoughts, and as influential on their imaginations, as film and television are today. Two passages from early literature illuminate this idea. The first is a preface to a poem in the *Man'yōshū* that reads as follows in Ian Levy's translation.

> On the thirteenth day of the New Year, Tempyō 2 (730), a banquet was held at the estate of the venerable Ōtomo Tabito, Commander of the Dazaifu. The time was spring's splendid first month. The air was clear, the wind was soft. The plum blossoms opened like a spray of powder before a dressing mirror, and the orchids gave off a fragrance as from a purse of perfume. Not only that, but clouds shifted over the dawn peaks, and the pines were covered with a fine silk as they trailed their canopies. Fog thickened in the mountain hollows, and birds trapped in its silky crepe wandered lost in the woods. In the garden were butterflies fluttering anew, and in the sky were geese from the old year returning north. Here we were, with the sky our canopy and the earth our seat, knee to knee, our wine cups flying back and forth. We were all together, and our harmony was such that we forgot the need for speech. Facing the clouds and mist that stretch out beyond us, we all opened our collars, each acting serenely as his heart desired, each taking a delighted fulfillment in his own thoughts. How could we express those emotions other than in the garden of writing?

In Chinese poetry are recorded works on the falling plum blossoms. What difference between ancient and modern times? Come, let us too fashion a few small verses singing of the plum blossoms in the garden.[13]

Here we see a group of men, sitting together in a garden, awed by the beauty of the garden, such as the plum trees; by the beauty of wild nature seen within the garden, like the butterflies flitting about; and also by the beauty of wild nature seen from the vantage point of the garden, like the geese flying overhead. Their reaction to all this is, of course, to compose poems. What follows the preface in the *Man'yōshū* are thirty-two poems on the theme of plums presumably written at this banquet.

The second passage from early literature that illuminates the idea that courtiers were disposed to write poems based on aspects of nature they saw in their gardens comes from the Yomogiu chapter of *Genji Monogatari*. Here we find a passage that relates how young people, in written correspondence with people they feel have the same sentiments as they do, express their feelings in terms of "trees and grasses." In other words, they express their emotions and desires in terms of images of the natural world — both those taken from wild nature and those found in the garden.[14]

Classical Japanese poetry, called *waka*, can be considered to be a form of "nature poetry" in that the poems almost always set the scene by incorporating a season and some element of the natural world: a plant, a bird, a landscape, and so on. Most of these elements had specific symbolic meanings, acting as commonly understood links to other thoughts. In short, Heian-period poetry was based on images of nature, those images were in turn symbolic of other things, and those symbolisms were well-known to the courtiers of the day.

Gardens were not as central to the lives of Heian-period courtiers as poetry was. Everyone, it can be assumed, needed to have some education in and affinity with poetry but not everyone designed or owned a garden.

That said, any residence of any standing in the capital would have had a garden and courtiers of lesser rank who did not personally own large urban estates with highly developed gardens would have had frequent opportunities to see them during social visits to other residences. Garden design, like poetry, was based on the incorporation of scenes distilled from the natural world. Rather than following a geometric patterning or some other mathematical or architectural basis for the garden design, these scenes were quite naturalistic. Abstracted to be sure, but the aesthetics of their design were very much based on the rhythms and balances found in the natural world.

The connection between poetry and these gardens was threefold: understanding, design, and appreciation. To begin with, a garden would be designed based on images of wild nature. A courtier's understanding of the natural world, in turn, was informed by his knowledge of poetry. While it is true that courtiers would make short trips out of the capital itself into the meadows and low hills that surrounded the city, either to view the changing seasons or to make a pilgrimage to a local shrine or temple, they rarely made trips of any great distance unless they were required to by being posted to a distant province or exiled from court (although the former was often considered to be the latter). So, for the people of the court, poetry and travel tales — whether spoken or written — were their windows onto the natural world. They may never have actually laid eyes on pine trees along a wave-battered rocky seacoast but they certainly would have known the image from poems they had heard or read. What's more, even if they did travel, courtiers would not have made visual records while out in the natural world. Paper was a luxury item, so the kinds of sketch pads that artists haul around these days were unthinkable to the Heian-period courtier. When the courtiers thought of the natural world, the scenes they came up with in their minds were, at least in part, built from images that had been embedded in the well-known, classical poems they had read since childhood.

The second connection between poetry and gardens came during the design stage. Garden design was not done on paper with scaled drawings as it is today, for the same reason that people didn't make sketches. Paper was too precious. Instead, it was part of an ongoing process that took place as the garden was being made. When courtiers took on the task of designing the gardens of their residences, or when they were assisting other, most likely higher-level, courtiers with the designs of theirs, their choice of design elements was certain to be informed by the body of poetry they knew. If they chose to set rough boulders along the water's edge with pines hanging over them, they may well have been remembering a poem about a rocky seacoast, *ariso*, rather than a visit to such a seacoast. When choosing to plant clusters of sweet rush, *ayame*, in the shallows, it may well have been the *ayame* of poetry they were thinking of, rather than *ayame* they had seen in a stream or pond. Their choice of those elements of nature, and others, was very likely to have been shaped by poetic passages that incorporated those elements; and the scenic image they were recreating in the garden may well have been one that had first been imprinted on their minds upon hearing a poem.

Kamo no Chōmei (鴨長明, 1155–1216), a hermit poet who lived during the late Heian and early Kamakura periods, touches on this idea in his literary critique called the *Mumyōshō* (無名抄), in which he specifically compares the making of poetry with that of a garden. He writes, "To make a garden, we place rocks close to the spots where we plan to plant pines, and where we plan to dig a pond and set water running in streams we construct an artificial mountain which can further beautify the view. In the same way, we improve the configuration of a poem through our use of the names of famous places. Knowledge of how to use them constitutes one of the most important of the elements in our poetic heritage."[15] Of course, Chōmei was not saying "we build our gardens the way we write our poetry," he expressed it the other way around. But his juxtaposition of the two ideas — garden making and poetry writing — shows that the two endeavors were considered to be similar and comparable.

The third connection between poetry and gardens brings us back to the scene of Genji and Murasaki, namely, the appreciation of a garden. Even if a courtier had not been involved in its design, when he looked at a garden — because the gardens were built out of various images from nature — it was sure to evoke in his mind memories of famous poems that incorporated those images. That a courtier would see dew-drops on lotus leaves, or bent frost-withered grasses, or a bush clover drooping under the weight of morning dew, or sweet rush growing in the shallows of a pond, or a warbler flitting through plums in the garden, and not immediately be reminded of the specific symbolic imagery that was linked to each of those things in poems seems unlikely if not unthinkable. These images were simply too well-known to be missed.

Poetry and gardens were linked in these three ways — how nature was understood, how it was interpreted when gardens were designed, and how gardens were observed — and what follows in this book, after a brief introduction to poetry and gardens in the Heian period, are examples of poetic themes that were also used as design elements in the gardens, something we know from a variety of sources: literary, painterly, and archeological. These examples are presented here not only to give an understanding of how courtiers viewed their gardens in Japan a thousand years ago (an interesting but perhaps distant subject) but also to suggest that it is still possible to consider garden design and poetry as linked arts, even today. That it is still possible to hear the songs in the garden.

Heian-period Poetry

Japanese poetry of the classical era encompasses those poems that were written down during the Nara period (710–784) through the end of the Heian period (794–1185). A general term for these poems is *waka* (和歌), literally Japanese poems, and although there are various forms of *waka* of varying lengths, all the poems in this book are short poems called *tanka* (短歌), as opposed to longer poems known as *chōka* (長歌). These poems had certain identifying characteristics, some related to the form of the poems and some to their content.

The form of *tanka* is very distinctive. They were broken into five distinct sections (called *ku*) each with a specific, fixed syllable count: 5/7/5/7/7. Since the Japanese language is composed entirely of discrete syllables composed of either a single vowel (*a, i, u, e, o*) or a consonant followed by a vowel (*ka, ki, ku, ke, ko*, and so on), this poetic style fits the language very well. In addition, although there were five syllabic sections, those sections were thought of as being arranged in two parts or three parts. From ancient times until the Nara period, the most common pattern of breaking the poem was a format called *goshichichō* (literally five-seven tempo) which went as follows: 5/7 5/7/7. An alternate, 5/7 5/7 7 was also possible. The examples that follow in this book from the *Man'yōshū* are in the former pattern,

From the Heian period onward, however, the pattern became 5/7/5 7/7, although in some rare instances sections would contain an extra syllable, a condition referred to as *ji-amari*, literally *excess-letter*. *Gosen Wakashū* 1298 in the section on Araiso is one example. Despite these anomalies, 5/7/5   7/7 is the most common and widely understood patterning of *tanka* presently. The first three sections (5/7/5) make up an introduction called the *kami-no-ku*, upper section, and the following two sections (7/7) make up the *shimo-no-ku*, lower section or closure. During the Heian period, *kami-no-ku* and *shimo-no-ku* were referred to, respectively, as the *moto* (meaning *origin* or *beginning*, 本) and *sue* (meaning, *finish* or *closing*, 末). Typically, the introduction would present a certain symbolic poetic element and the closure would contain a reference to that element or a poetic play on it. Regarding the content of the poems, there were a number of poetic devices used to add symbolic meaning to the poems. These devices were primarily words, or short phrases, that were linked poetically to other words or phrases in a pre-determined manner so that one led naturally into the other. Through the use of these devices, even a relatively short poem such as a *tanka* could be made very complex, as each short section of the poem was encoded with linked and layered meanings. These poetic devices included *makura-kotoba*, *kake-kotoba*, *uta-makura*, and *engo*.

A *makura-kotoba*, literally "pillow word," is a standard epithet used in a poem that sets the ground for, and points toward, an associated word or phrase that will follow, usually immediately afterwards. *Makura-kotoba* are usually five syllables in length and typically appear in the first section of a *tanka*. One example is the phrase *karu kaya no*. *Karu* means to cut with a sickle, *kaya* referred to any grass that was harvested for a specific purpose such as roofing material, and *no* can be a possessive particle (*of* cut grasses), a comparitive article (*like* cut grasses), or a subject marker (*these* cut grasses). *Karu-kaya* was also a set phrase that referred to any tall grasses that were used for utilitarian purposes, so *karu kaya no* may refer either to the scene of grasses that *have been* cut, or to a meadow of tall grasses of the type that *would be* cut. When grasses are cut with a sickle, they fall about in all directions in a scattered state. Likewise, those tall grasses, when beaten about by strong winds, create a scene of mayhem even if they are not cut. For both reasons, the expression *karu kaya no* became linked to the image of scattered confusion, which is the basis of the *makura-kototoba*. When readers of a poem come upon the expression *karu kaya no*, they expect that it will be followed by the word *midaru*, to be confused, or *omoimidaru*, to have a confused state of mind. An example of a poem that contains this particular *makura-kotoba* is this from the *Man'yōshū*.[16]

万葉集　3065
み吉野の　秋津の小野に　刈る草の　思ひ乱れて　寝る夜しそ多き
miyoshino no　akizu no ono ni　karu kaya no　omoi midarete　nuru yo shiso ōki

> *Man'yōshū*　3065
> In beautiful Yoshino
> 　　the dragonfly fields of Akizu
> 　　　　are strewn with cut grasses
> My thoughts scatter as wildly
> 　　troubling many an evening's sleep

Another example of a *makura-kotoba* is the phrase *momiji ba no*. *Momiji* can refer either to the Japanese maple tree, which makes a show of beautiful fall colors, or to autumn colors in general. *Momiji ba no* thus translates either as "leaves of the maple tree" or "leaves of autumn colors," and because coloring leaves so clearly mark the turning of the seasons, *momiji ba no* links to words such as *sugu*, to pass. The following poem uses the connection to *sugu* to accentuate the passing of the seasons as well as the passing of a beloved person.[17]

万葉集　47
軽皇子、安騎の野に宿る時に、柿本朝臣人麻呂の作る歌
ま草刈る　荒野にはあれど　黄葉の　過ぎにし君が　形見とそ来し
ma kusa karu　arano ni wa aredo　momichi ba no　suginishi kimi ga　katami to so koshi

Man'yōshū 47

>Kakinomoto no Hitomaro
>
>When Prince Karu lodged on the fields of Akino

>Although this is but a wild moor
>>where we come only to harvest the rich grasses
>>>we gather now in memory
>
>The brocade of autumn colors
>>and our Prince, now passed[18]

The second device used in *tanka* to allow for symbolic connections is called a *kake-kotoba*, or pivot word. The *kake-kotoba* is a pun based on homonyms. A word that could have two or more meanings is placed somewhere in the middle of a poem. When read within the context of what comes before it, the word has one meaning. When read as part of what follows, it has another meaning and thus acts as a "pivot" in the middle of the poem. When the Japanese language is written using *kanji*, Chinese script, each character has one or more fixed meanings. When it is written using *hiragana*, which is a syllabary, only the word's sound and not its meaning is recorded. By using *hiragana* to write the *kake-kotoba*, the poet could avoid pinning down the word's exact meaning. Likewise, when a poem was sung out loud — listened to and not read — its meaning was also open to interpretation.

One example of a *kake-kotoba* is found in poem 617 of the *Kokinshū* that revolves around the word *nagame*. *Nagame* is the contracted form of *naga-ame* which means a "long rain." It can also be interpreted as a form of the verb *nagamu*, which means "to gaze upon" in modern Japanese and, in the Heian period, had the additional meaning of "to ponder over deeply" or "to think back upon with fondness."[19]

古今和歌集　617
　　藤原敏行
　　なりひらの朝臣の家に侍りける女のもとによみてつかはしける

つれづれの　ながめにまさる　涙河　袖のみ濡れて　逢ふよしもなし
tsurezure no　nagame ni masaru　namidagawa　sode nomi nurete　au yoshi mo nashi

　　Kokin Wakashū 617
　　　Fujiwara no Toshiyuki
　　　Sent to a woman in the house of Narihira no Ason

　　Only my sleeves soak
　　　　with a river of tears　　stronger
　　　　　　than the endless flowing rains
　　I linger helplessly　　thinking of you
　　　　all hope of meeting gone

Another example of a *kake-kotoba* can be found in poem number 1165 in the *Senzai Wakashū*. This one pivots around the word *fumi* that can mean a "letter" or "writings" if interpreted one way, or can mean "to step upon" if interpreted another way. This poem, by the way, is an unusual *sedōka*, having one extra verse of 5 syllables.[20]

千載和歌集　　1165
　　源俊頼朝臣

かきたえし　真間の継橋　ふみ見れば　隔てたる　霞も晴れて　向かへるがごと
kakitaeshi　mama no tsugi hashi　fumi mireba　hedatetaru　kasumi mo harete　mukaeru ga goto[21]
　　Senzai Wakashū 1165
　　　Minamoto no Toshiyori no Ason

My letters broke off   yes
        but just seeing yours
                and it's as if I'm stepping across
        the plank bridges at the Mama inlet
        The mists of distance lift
                and we meet — together once more

The third device used in poetry is called an *uta-makura*, the literal translation of which is "poem pillow." *Uta-makura* are the names of famous places that were so deep in history and meaning that their introduction into a poem, being instantly recognizable and connected to some aspect of history or culture, would enrich and enliven the work. In the aforementioned passage in which Kamo no Chōmei said, "We improve the configuration of a poem through our use of the names of famous places," it was *uta-makura* he was referring to and the "plank bridges at the Mama inlet," *Mama no tsugihashi*, in the poem just introduced is one such *uta-makura*.

Another example of a place that was famously connected to a poetic theme and became an *uta-makura* was the village of Ide, which lay south of Heian-kyō. That village was known for the kerria shrubs, *yamabuki*, that grew along the banks of the streams there, and the little river frogs that clambered among the rocks, as depicted in this poem from the *Kokinshū*.[22]

古今和歌集　125
　よみ人しらず

かはづ鳴く　井手の山吹　散りにけり　花のさかりに　あはましものを
kawazu naku　ide no yamabuki　chirinikeri　hana no sakari ni　awamashi mono wo

　Kokin Wakashū 125
　Anonymous

The sweet river frog cries
  among the scattered blossoms
    of *yamabuki* near Ide village
 Too late would that I had caught them
  in cascades of full bloom

Another example of an *uta-makura*, perhaps the quintessential example, is the association of the place known as Yoshino (or Miyoshino, Beautiful Yoshino) with cherry blossoms. Of all the poetic themes linked to place names, this one was certain to be known to any literate person. [23]

古今和歌集　60
　紀友則
　寛平御時きさいの宮の哥合のうた

みよし野の　山辺にさける　桜花　雪かとのみぞ　あやまたれける
miyoshino no　yamabe ni sakeru　sakurabana　yuki ka to nomi zo　ayamatarekeru

 Kokin Wakashū 60
  Ki no Tomonori
  From a poetry contest in the Kanpyō Era

Cherry trees
  burst in full bloom among the mountains
    of Yoshino
Misled by their beauty
  seeing only drifts of snow

The fourth and final poetic device to be introduced is called *engo*. These are associative words that link two words in the poem through some relationship. This association can happen in one of two ways. The first is that the words in question are homonyms, and their similar sounds link them naturally even though they have different meanings. In the second method, the two words are not homonyms but they are so commonly understood as being associated with each other, that the link between the two flows naturally.

An example of the former, in which the *engo* is based on homonyms, would be the word *yo*, which can have several meanings. A poem using this particular *engo* will include the phrase *take no fushi*, or some variant of that. *Take* is bamboo, and *fushi* is the growth node along the stem of the bamboo. The spaces between the nodes on the stem are called *yo*. So the expression *take no fushi* immediately brings to mind the idea of *yo*, even without mentioning the word directly. In this case, *yo* is written with the Chinese character 節 (as is *fushi*). The word *yo*, however, can also mean "the world" or "society," as well as refer to the relations between men and women (being "worldly"), when written with the character 世, and can mean "generations" when written 代. Thus, the introduction of the phrase *take no fushi*, bamboo nodes, into a poem is associatively linked to comments that follow in the poem on the ways of the world, the troubled nature of society, or the ongoing flow of time. The following is from the *Kokinshū*.[24]

古今和歌集　957
　　よみ人知らず
　　物思ひける時、いときなきこを見てよめる

　いまさらに　なに生ひいづらむ　竹の子の　優き節しげき　よtとは知らずや

　imasara ni　nani oiizuramu　take no ko no　uki fushi shigeki　yo to wa shirazu ya

Kokin Wakashū 957

Anonymous

Composed upon seeing an innocent child at a time when
I was filled with worry

At such a time as this
why were you born at all
Rising into a world as filled with grief
as the countless nodes
on a bamboo shoot

A second example of *engo*, this one based on a non-homophonic pairing of words, is the association between the words *ura* (浦), which means a bay or cove by the ocean, and *ariso* (荒磯), which is a rough, rocky seacoast. *Ariso* is pronounced *ara-iso* in modern Japanese, but in classical poetry we usually find the expression contracted to three syllables, except when four syllables are rhythmically required as in the expression, "*araiso no.*" For anyone who had traveled along the coast of Japan by the small ships that hugged the shoreline up and down the Inland Sea, the image of coves and bays lined with rocky shores would have been well known. For those who didn't travel far from home, and that was most of the courtiers, this image was known through travel stories and poems. Poem 631 from the *Shūi Wakashū* captures this *engo* beautifully.[25]

拾遺和歌集　631

かくてのみ　ありその浦の　浜千鳥　よそに鳴きつゝ　恋ひやわたらむ
kakute nomi　ariso no ura no　hamachidori　yoso ni nakitsutsu　koi ya wataramu

Shūi Wakashū 631

It's come down to this
    sitting on the rocks of the bay
        so far from anywhere
Can love last   crying endlessly
    the lonely plover and me

Makura-kotoba, kake-kotoba, uta-makura, and *engo*: not all *tanka* necessarily employed these specific techniques but almost all poems evoked a meaning greater than the superficial statement given in their thirty-one syllables. Since the imagery in poems, being based on nature, so often overlapped that found in the gardens, it is easy to surmise that the garden acted as a constant source of "trigger images" like Genji's dew-drop jewels. These elements in the garden would evoke memories of known poems or urge a person with literary sentiments to compose a new poem. It may be that some of the courtiers found poetry, and the poetic images interwoven in the garden, to be deeply moving in the truest sense. The references to passion, grief, loneliness, desire, and world-weariness depicted in the poems touched them and caused them to sigh, or cry, or smile. It may also be that some courtiers were not moved by poetry. They may have found those same poetic images to be trite, stereotypic, and false. But whether they were moved by the poems or not, the symbolic meaning of the images in the poems, and those in the gardens, would not have gone unnoticed.

Poetry Sources

The poems presented in this book were taken from the following anthologies. Some of these, like the *Man'yōshū* and *Kokinshū*, were well-known to courtiers during the Heian period as evidenced by their appearance in diaries that record the on-goings at court, or in critical reviews of poetry.[26] All of them however, were chosen because they were compiled before or during the Heian period, and the poems contained within them, having been considered to be important works at that time, were very likely to have been well-known to the courtier society.

Gosen Wakashū 後撰和歌集 *The Later Anthology of Japanese Poems,* also known as *Gosenshū*, was compiled in 951 by five court poets known as the Five Men of the Pear Chamber (梨壺の五人, *Nashitsubo no gonin*) at the request of Emperor Murakami (r. 946–967). *Gosenshū* is noted for the many poems that have introductory prose statements which set the scene for the poem. It contains over 1,400 poems in twenty thematic sections, covering the various seasons, love, and miscellany. The name "*Later*" derives from the fact that many of the poems were selected from those that were considered for but rejected from inclusion in the *Kokinshū*.

Goshūi Wakashū 後拾遺和歌集 *The Later Gleanings: Anthology of Japanese Poems,* also known as *Goshūishū*, compiled by Fujiwara no Michitoshi (1047–1099) in 1086 at the request of Emperor Shirakawa (r. 1073–1087). It contains over 1,200 poems in twenty thematic sections of

FUJI

towanu ma wo
uramurasaki ni
aku fuji no
nani tote matsu ni
kakarisomekemu
Shika Wakashū 257

WISTERIA

For so long I have heard nothing
I flower   a deep-lavender wisteria
yet am resentful, bitter
Why on earth did I cling
to that pine of mine

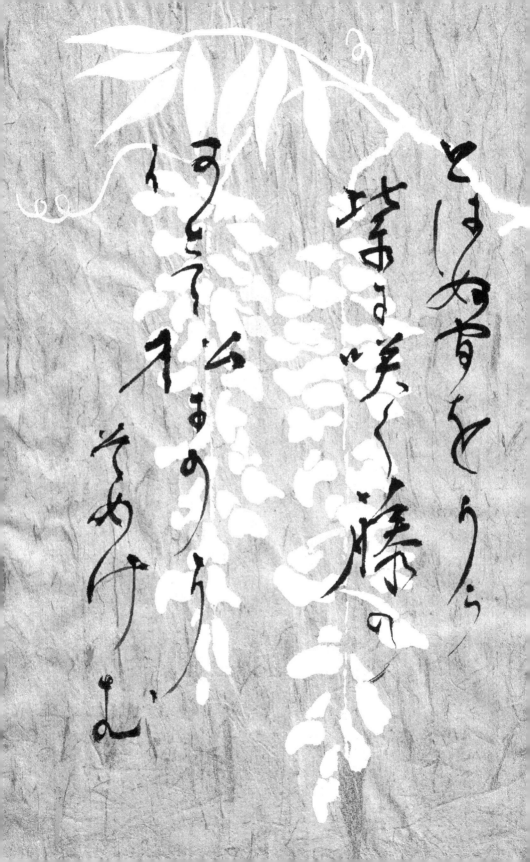

とまぬ昔をうら
塔を咲く藤の
はつて私まのう
さめけむ

the various seasons, love, and so on, many of which were written by women poets. The name, *Goshūishū, Later Gleanings*, stems from the fact that it follows after *Shūishū*.

Ise Monogatari 伊勢物語 *The Tales of Ise* is a Japanese collection of *tanka* poems and associated narratives, dating from the Heian period. The current version comprises 125 sections, with each combining poems and prose, giving a total of 209 poems in most versions. The exact date of composition and authorship can only be speculated on; the identity of the nameless, idealized central character is likewise ambiguous, but suggested to be Ariwara no Narihira (825–880). Thirty of the poems from *The Tales of Ise* that appear in the *Kokin Wakashū* (905) with similar head notes are all attributed to Narihira. The combination of these poems, and the similarity of some events in the tales to Narihira's life, have led to the additional suggestion that Narihira actually composed the work; however, the inclusion of material and events dating after 880 suggests otherwise.

Kin'yō Wakashū 金葉和歌集 *Golden Leaves: Anthology of Japanese Poems*, also known as *Kin'yōshū*, complied by Minamoto no Toshiyori (1055?–1129) by 1127 at the request of Retired Emperor Shirakawa. A short anthology, it contains over 700 poems in only ten thematic volumes.

Kokin Wakashū 古今和歌集 *Anthology of Ancient and Modern Japanese Poems*, also known as *Kokinshū*, complied by court poets, including Ki no Tsurayuki. The *Kokinshū* was commissioned by Emperor Daigo (r. 897–930) and completed by around 920. It contains over 1,100 poems in twenty thematic sections: spring, summer, travel, love, and so on.

Man'yōshū 万葉集 *Anthology of Ten Thousand Leaves*, an anthology of poems compiled in the Nara period (710--794) containing more than 4,500 poems of various types — mostly *chōka*, *tanka*, and *sedōka* — by authors that span over 350 years. The collection is partitioned into twenty non-thematic volumes. The compiler was purportedly Ōtomo no Yakamochi (717?–785), although he may have been only the last in a series of compilers. The *Man'yōshū* is the oldest collection of Japanese poetry and easily the most famous.

Murasaki Shikibu Shū 紫式部集   *Collected Poems of Murasaki Shikibu*. Murasaki Shikibu (紫式部; c. 973–c. 1014 or 1025), or Lady Murasaki as she is often known in English, was a palace attendant of the imperial court during the Heian period. She was a poet and is best known as the author of *Genji Monogatari, The Tale of Genji*, written in Japanese between about 1000 and 1008, one of the earliest extant novels in the world. Murasaki Shikibu was not her real name, which is unknown. Some scholars have postulated that her given name might have been Fujiwara Takako, recorded as the name of a lady-in-waiting ranked *naishi no jō* on the 29th day of the 1st month, Kankō 4 (February 19, 1007), according to *Midō Kampaku Ki,* a diary written by Fujiwara no Michinaga. Her own diary, the *Murasaki Shikibu Nikki, Diary of Murasaki Shikibu*, suggests that she was nicknamed Murasaki (purple) at court, after a character in her own work, *The Tale of Genji. Shikibu* is a title that refers to her father's position in the Bureau of Ceremony (*shikibu-shō*).

Sanka Wakashū 山家和歌集 *Mountain Home Anthology of Japanese Poems*, also known as *Sankashū*, comprises the poems written by the hermit-monk and poet, Saigyō (1118–1190), during his lifetime. It contains over 1,500 poems in several thematic sections.

Senzai Wakashū 千載和歌集 *Thousand Year Anthology of Japanese Poems*, also known as *Senzaishū*, compiled by Fujiwara no Shunzei (1114–1204) by 1187 at the request of the Retired Emperor Go-Shirakawa. (r. 1155–1158). It contains over 1,200 poems in twenty thematic volumes.

Shika Wakashū 詞花和歌集, the *Poem Flowers Anthology of Japanese Poems*, also known as *Shikashū*, compiled by Fujiwara no Akisuke (1090–1155) by 1144 at the request of Emperor Sutoku (r. 1123–1141). Even shorter than *Kin'yōshū*, it contains only slightly over 400 poems in ten thematic volumes.

Shūi Wakashū 拾遺和歌集 *The Gleanings: Anthology of Japanese Poems*, also known as *Shūishū*, compiled by an unknown person around 1005–1007. It contains over 1,300 poems in twenty thematic sections on the various seasons, love, and so on. The name, *Gleanings*, comes from the fact that the poems were "gleaned" from those not included in either the *Kokinshū* or *Gosenshū*.

Tsurayukishū 貫之集 *The Collected Writings of Tsurayuki*. Ki no Tsurayuki (872–945) was a Heian-period courtier and poet. He is perhaps best known as one of the compilers of, and contributors to, the *Kokinshū*. He is the editor, mentioned earlier, who wrote the Japanese preface of the *Kokinshū* that begins, "The poetry of Yamato is like a seed in the heart of our people, which has unfurled as myriad-leaved songs." He also wrote a travel diary, the *Tosa Nikki*, which he writes in the voice of a woman. *Tsurayukishū*, is an anthology of the poems he wrote and was presumably compiled by him.

Heian-period Garde.

Gardens were built in both Buddhist temples and private residences during the Heian period but this book focuses on those found in residences, specifically on those gardens that were built on the urban estates of imperial courtiers. Their properties were rectangular plots defined by the grid-like streets of the city. A top-ranking aristocrat received a plot of one *chō* in size: a square of 120 meters by 120 meters (about 130 yards by 130 yards). Lesser courtiers received a half *chō*, a quarter *chō,* or less. The entire plot was typically surrounded by a high, thick rammed-earth wall. The residential structure was of a wooden post and beam architecture, raised some 60 cm to 1 meter (two to three feet) off the ground for air circulation. Some of the walls were removable panels and the roof was large and over-hanging to provide summer shade. The main hall sat in the middle of the site, facing south, and other ancillary halls surrounded it to the east, north, and west, connected to one another by roofed corridors. To the south was a broad open area spread with sand that was used for outdoor gatherings and performances. Further to the south, between the open area and the outer wall, was the garden. This is a stereotypic description but every literary and painterly document and all archeological evidence from that era confirm this layout. The garden often had as a central element an irregularly shaped pond fed by a meandering stream, artificial hills, and a variety of plantings.

The clearest description of the gardens from that time is found in a book on garden building called the *Sakuteiki*, or *Records of Garden Making.* The *Sakuteiki* introduces thoughts on garden-making in topical sections such as ponds and islands, stones, gardening styles, waterfalls, garden streams, taboos, and trees. The material presented can be said to cover five main thematic areas: technical advice, nature, geomancy, Buddhism, and taboos. The technical advice ranges from giving specific elevations and dimensions for the design of the garden to describing how to keep a wellspring of underground feed pipe from leaking by packing it with clay. Nature is presented as being the basic template for garden design. The reader is admonished to pay strict attention to natural rhythms and forms and recreate them in the garden, for instance, in the shape of a stream or waterfall. Even the position that a stone had when it was found in nature — upright, horizontal, or tilted at an angle — was purposefully recreated when that stone was brought to the city and set in a garden. Geomancy is a Chinese system of geo-physics that was used to guide all manner of design, from gardens to cities. It was based on the understanding and interpretation of two interrelated systems: the Five Phases, and Yin and Yang.[27] Buddhism was also incorporated into garden design. Some elements of the gardens, such as tall waterfalls or triptych arrangements of standing stones, were seen as enshrining Buddhist deities. Finally, taboos that governed the daily habits of the courtiers — from deciding on when to wash their hair to which direction to travel on a particular day — also affected the design of the garden. A garden that ignored these taboos was destined to cause illness and social or financial failure for the residents.

Extrapolating from the *Sakuteiki* and other sources, we can surmise that the building and use of a garden by a Heian-period courtier would have gone something like this. The designer would walk about the area of land to the south of the main residence hall that was enclosed by the sturdy surrounding earthen wall, *tsuijibei*, to get a sense of the lay of the land and try to capture some essence of the spirit of the place, *fuzei*. Thinking over scenes of wild nature and extant gardens built by skilled designers, he would come up with a plan for the garden that may include a central pond, streams running into and out of the pond, hill forms in the background, a flat, open area in the foreground for festive gatherings, and meadow-like areas to the sides. The size of the gathering area — in other words the distance between the residence and the pond — was determined by the social rank of the garden owner, hence the number of visitors he might be expected to entertain.

The shape of a pond would be marked out with stakes. Using a water-level (a shallow tray with water in it), elevations would be marked on the stakes so that the water level of the finished pond was known in advance. This would allow the shaping of the pond edges to be done properly. The soil in the pond area was then dug out, and used to make the islands in the pond or the hill-forms. Men would be sent out from the household to the hills and river valleys surrounding the capital to search for stones of various sizes and shapes. These would include small, fist-sized river pebbles used to line the bottoms of the streams and the pond, all the way up to boulders that required one or two carts to carry them. The stones would be brought back to the construction site in the city and laid out in such a way as to have them visible to the person overseeing the project who could then select them at will. Stones intended to be used as standing stones would be temporarily set standing up; those that would be used horizontally would be laid out lying down, and so on.

The main stones in the garden design would be set out first, putting them on top of small stones that had been pounded into the soil as foundation stones. After those initial stones were set, all the other stones in the design would be placed following in accordance with the first ones or, in the parlance of the day, following "the request of the main stones." Along with the pond, the streams and hills would be finished in the same manner — the soil rough-shaped, then the main stones set, and then the secondary stones set in among them.

After the soil-work and stone-work were completed, men would be sent out again to areas surrounding the capital to search for plants, including trees such as pines and maples, shrubs like bush clover and azalea, and grasses and perennials such as silver grass and chrysanthemums. The plants would be dug up and brought back to the garden. Some smaller plants, such as perennial flowers, and even shrubs like bush clover, were planted as seeds collected from the wild or from other gardens. In this way, the garden would be developed through earth-work, stone-setting, and plantings into thematic regions representing the ocean, rivers, mountains, or wetlands, while following the prescriptions of geomantic rules and social taboos.

Garden Sources

Regarding how it was determined that certain poetic elements — pine trees, irises, streams, and so on — were also found in the gardens of the Heian period, specific explanations will be given with each entry. As a general introduction, there were basically two kinds of sources: archeological evidence and literary evidence. Many archeological digs have been completed on gardens from the Heian period and earlier. In some rare cases, those gardens were restored, but most were reburied or destroyed by new construction after thorough examination. These research findings have revealed very accurately the placement of stones in the gardens and the shape of ponds and streams. As for plant materials, although the living plants have long since disappeared, advanced archeological techniques can find evidence of specific plants in tiny scraps of leaves, seeds, cones, fruit pits, bark, and even pollen. Of course, the finer the material, the higher the possibility that the plant may not have been *in* the garden but only *near* the garden and that the evidence was introduced by the wind.

As far as literary evidence, the above mentioned *Sakuteiki* is one very clear source of information. Then there are the diaries, *nikki*, of Heian-period courtiers who noted down, often with an unforgiving eye and pithy wit, the daily events of the time, as well as fictional tales called *monogatari*. What the authors recorded was determined primarily by their personal interests. For Sei Shōnagon and Murasaki Shikibu, who were women at court, this means that we find a surprising number of comments in their writings about the various goings-on of court society and, of course, fashion. There are numerous comments on the colors of clothing worn, the patterns of the textiles, and so on. Gardens are not the main focus of these books, but neither are they never mentioned. In *Genji Monogatari*, for instance, glimpses of the gardens — the flora and fauna, waterways and stones — show up in many ways in almost every chapter. Of course, these works are all fictional accounts — even the diaries must be regarded as such. So one cannot say for a fact that because Prince Genji did something in his garden — released crickets into the grasses to hear their evocative cries, for instance — that it was actually so in reality. However, since the interest of the authors of these accounts was primarily to record the ongoings of their lives and the lives of other people of their community, the small references they made to things seen in the gardens were less likely to be the object of purposeful fictionalization. In any case, the combination of all the evidence — literary, painterly, and archeological — merges to provide a list of very likely candidates for this study, namely, elements of nature that were found in both gardens and poems. The literary sources include the following:

Sakuteiki 作庭記 *Records of Garden Making*, written in the mid-11th century in Japan. The authorship of the *Sakuteiki* is attributed to Tachibana no Toshitsuna (1028–1094), a court noble well-informed in the art of garden making, but this is only conjecture and the text may have been the combined work of several authors. The content was described in detail just above in The Heian Garden.

Genji Monogatari 源氏物語 *The Tale of Genji*, written in the early 11th century, the work is attributed to the Japanese noblewoman Murasaki

Shikibu. The book follows the fictional life at court of Prince Genji (and continues past his death) and offers many insights into the interest in poetry among courtiers as well as many glimpses of the gardens at courtier residences.

Makura no Sōshi 枕草子 *The Pillow Book*, written during the end of the 10th and beginning of the 11th centuries by Sei Shōnagon (清少納言, c. 966–1017), lady-in-waiting to Empress Teishi. *Makura no Sōshi* is a diary-like record of the ongoings at court offering many glimpses of court lifestyle, including the integration of poetry into court society and several views of the gardens as well.

Murasaki Shikibu Nikki 紫式部日記 *The Diary of Lady Murasaki*, covering several years in her life at the court of Empress Akiko from 1008 to 1010. Among the descriptions of everyday activities at court there are many scenes that reveal aspects of the residential gardens and how courtiers used them.

Eiga Monogatari 栄花物語 *Tales of Flowering Splendor*, is attributed to several possible authors over the course of the 11th century. The work records the exploits of nobleman Fujiwara no Michinaga against the backdrop of Heian court society, and captures some glimpses of the gardens he lived with.

Chiteiki 池亭記 *Record of a Pond Pavilion*. Written in the late 10th century by a court nobleman, Yoshishige no Yasutane (慶滋保胤, 931?–1002). The first part of two sections records the author's view of the decline of the capital. The second half records his life in seclusion and it is here that a few glimpses of his own garden appear.

Translating the Poems

As mentioned before, the poems presented in this book were written in the *tanka* form, in other words they had these distinctive features:

1) They were broken into five sections or breaths.

2) Each of those five sections had a fixed syllable count: 5/7/5/7/7.

3) The five sections were, in turn, separated into two sections: the aforementioned introduction, *kami-no-ku* (5/7/5), and closure, *shimo-no-ku* (7/7), or the older *goshichichō* (5/7 5/7/7).

4) The content of the poems was primarily based on nature imagery, which was used to convey the feelings of the poet in a symbolic manner.

5) The poems employed a number of poetic devices to add layered meaning to an otherwise brief poem. These included *makura-kotoba, kake-kotoba, uta-makura,* and *engo.*

It should be apparent that, when trying to make a translation between two languages as different as Japanese and English, it is all but impossible to maintain all five of the above aspects and still render a concise and beautiful poem. The question was, which aspects to favor.

The separation of the poem into five sections was an interesting issue. The original poems, in fact, were not written in five separate lines. Rather, they were written in one flowing line that broke wherever the size of the paper required, and since paper sheets were precious and small in the Heian period, that meant the lines broke in one or two random places. Although the poems were not *written* in separate lines, they were clearly *conceived of* in five separate sections and, when they were sung or chanted, this was done in five separate "breaths." So, breaking the poem into five lines helps convey the cadence of the poetry as it was sung.

The syllable count is something that could be maintained fairly easily. However, the strict patterning of 5/7/5/7/7 syllables, though certainly possible in English, is less elegant than in Japanese. The inherent staccato patterning of the Japanese language, in which each syllable is either a simple consonant/vowel combination (like *ka, ki, ku, ke, ko*), or at times just a vowel (*a, i, u, e, o*), lends a gracefully lyrical quality to what would otherwise be a very rigid structure. This meant maintaining a strict syllable count in English, although possible, was not given preference.

The separation of the entire poem into two sections — *kami-no-ku* and *shimo-no-ku* — was a fairly important aspect of the conceptual development of many of the poems. Ideas or concepts developed in the first introductory section would typically be played upon in the second closure section. Reflecting this two-part quality was considered to be of importance.

The aspect of these *tanka* to use nature imagery as the basis for expressing personal sentiments or feelings was, of course, not only essential to the poetry but also fundamental to the purpose of this book. These elements very much needed to be expressed in the translations.

And finally, there was the most difficult problem of the various poetic devices that add layered meaning to the poems. The interrelationships between these parts is often so complex that it takes paragraphs of footnotes to fully explain what is going on in a poem of thirty-one syllables. To capture all of the suggested meanings often becomes unfeasible. In the case of words that are homonyms, for instance, it is almost impossible to find two words in English that have the same meanings as the Japanese and are also homonyms. The word *matsu* is the rare exception that proves the case. In Japanese, *matsu* can mean both "a pine tree" and "to wait" for something. So an image of a pine on a rocky shore can be taken as a lonely person waiting for a lover to appear. You can approximate this in English by saying, "pining for one's lover," and yet, even this example falls short because in Japanese one can convey this feeling of waiting simply by mentioning the pine tree. And, it goes without saying, that other homonyms in Japanese have no English equivalents at all.

In the following poem from the *Kokinshū*, for instance, the word *ayame* is used twice which lends a rhythmic resonance to the poem. In the first instance *ayame* is the name for a plant called sweet rush. In the second instance, it means the pattern of woven cloth and appears as part of the expression, *ayame mo shiranu*, "cannot discern the pattern" or more figuratively, "can't distinguish between" or "is blind to." Obviously, there is no single word in English that means both "sweet rush" and "pattern," so this homonym cannot be translated directly.

古今和歌集　469

郭公　なく五月の　あやめぐさ　あやめも知らぬ　恋もするかな
hototogisu　naku ya satsuki no　ayamegusa　ayame mo shiranu　koi mo suru kana

> *Kokin Wakashū* 469
> Crying over the sweet rush
> in the rainy month of June
> The pattern beyond comprehension
> my love is but blind

Any of the words or phrases in these *tanka* may contain one or more historical, metaphorical, geographical, or seasonal references layered below the overt meaning of the poem. Trying to express the meaning of the original poem as well as all these literary associations is hard enough to do properly. Doing it within the 5/7/5/7/7 syllable pattern becomes limiting rather than helpful. As a result, the translations in this book give preference to three aspects of the original poems: the imagery of nature is intact, they are broken into five lines in two sections that reflect the rhythm of the poem when sung, and the overt and associative/symbolic meanings are expressed as poetically as possible.

Poetic Elements

Comments and Translations

Ame 雨 Rain

Rain, of course, needs no explanation, except to say how prevalent and consistent rain is in Japan. An archipelago that sits in the Pacific Ocean off the coast of the Asian continent, Japan is bathed by relatively warm ocean currents that flow up from the south and the warm moist winds that follow them. The result is rain. A lot of it. And, because of the regularity of the seasonal shifts, twice a year there are particularly rainy seasons. The first occurs around June, which would approximately be the 5th month in the calendar of the Heian period, and as can be expected, rain in the 5th month is an oft-repeated image in the poems. Rains and high winds also come again in September as the typhoons arrive to break the heat of summer. Again, cold autumn rains, often depicted with autumn winds, are a standard poetic metaphor.

Rain is life-giving and, in as much, all cultures rejoice in rain. Or so one would expect. The image of rain, however, that we get from Heian-period literature is somewhat different. There is little or no rejoicing when rain is mentioned. Instead, the reaction seems to fall primarily into two categories: boredom and dread. Sei Shōnagon, in her book *Makura no Sōshi*, epitomizes the former. One can imagine her languishing by the veranda, her lips in a pout, eyebrows knit in a frown, and railing against the weather that keeps her from going out. In fact, she lists heavy rain in her column of Boring Things as being the "boringest thing ever."[28] The expression used for "boring" in this case is *tsurezure,* which can be translated as tedium or idleness. As we will discuss further below, *ame* is often connected to *tsurezure* in poems.

The other depiction of rain is not so mellow. As rain falls from heaven, we find that the two concepts are linked. Heaven in this case does not mean "that place where one goes when one dies" but rather "the heavens," the place where the gods reside and where the fate of mortal beings is determined. That being so, one does not fool with heaven, and something that falls from heaven is just as likely to bring bad luck as good. Sei Shōnagon's reluctance to go out in the long rains of summer was not just because she didn't want to get her clothing muddy (although that may have been a big part of it in her case), but because getting rained on was considered to be a sure way to ruin one's luck. The Hahakigi chapter of *Genji Monogatari* begins by noting how the summer rains went on endlessly and the palace was in seclusion due to taboos.[29] We often find these two concepts — *ame*, rain, and *mono-imi*, a taboo — presented close together even if not directly, causatively linked.

In Gardens

Despite the negative connotations, rain was essential to Heian-period gardens. The falling rain watered the plantings, brightening the moss and other greenery, and fed the streams, waterfalls, and ponds that were fundamental to the design. In fact, the high degree of precipitation in Japan allows for the broad horticultural palette and distinctive patinas that one finds in the gardens there. The garden seen filtered through strands of raindrops or still covered with beads of water after a rain had lifted, the sound of falling rain on leaves in the garden, these are all things that became part of the aesthetics of the garden.

In Poetry

There are several standard conceptual links associated with *ame*. Those mentioned already are the seasonal links between rain and the 5th month and autumn. The first depicts warm summer rains, sweet rush (*ayame*), and singing cuckoo birds (*hototogisu*), while the latter might evoke cold rains over meadows of windswept bush clover (*hagi*) or trees turning red and gold (*momiji*).

Another use in poetry, also mentioned above, is the link between rain and boredom. The restrictions placed on the people of the court that forced them to sit idle in the rain also kept them from visiting their lovers. In poems that refer to situations like these, the word *ame* is linked with *tsurezure*, idleness.

A third usage is the *kake-kotoba*, *nagame*. *Nagame* means "to gaze upon" or "to reflect thoughtfully upon," but it can also be heard as a contraction of *naga-ame*, "long rain." One can easily sense the associations inherent between the feelings of sitting inside, gazing out at the garden, waiting for a rain that continues without end for days and days to stop. One example can be found in the poem from *Kokinshū* that follows.

Another link is found in the word *kawa* meaning river which is an *engo* with *ame*. The link here seems obvious — rains fall, rivers run — but in fact in poetry there is often one deeper layer connecting the rains with a river, in this case a river of tears from someone crying over a lost love.

The last poetic convention is not related to the word *ame*, but to the words *furu* and *furi*, which can mean "fall" — as in "the rain falls" — but also can mean "to age" or "to elapse." Some poems, as with the second example from the *Kokinshū* that follows, use that similarity to create a link between the images of rain and of aging.

古今和歌集　617
　　藤原敏行
　　なりひらの朝臣の家に侍りける女のもとによみてつかはしける

つれづれの　ながめにまさる　涙河　袖のみぬれて　逢ふよしもなし
tsurezure no　nagame ni masaru　namidagawa　sode nomi nurete　au yoshi mo nashi

> *Kokin Wakashū* 617
> 　　Fujiwara no Toshiyuki
> 　　Sent to a woman in the house of Narihira no Ason
>
> Only my sleeves soak
> 　　with a river of tears　　stronger
> 　　　　than the endless flowing rains
> I linger helplessly　thinking of you
> 　　all hope of meeting gone

ॐ　　　ॐ

古今和歌集　782
　　をののこまち　　（小野小町）

今はとて　わが身時雨に　ふりぬれば　言の葉さへに　移ろひにけり
ima wa tote　waga mi shigure ni　furinureba　koto no ha sae ni　utsuroinikeri

> *Kokin Wakashū* 782
> 　　Ono no Komachi
>
> The end is near
> 　　Everything fading　　the leaves　　my body
> 　　　　as cold as these showers
> Even the words you send my way
> 　　are as autumn leaves

Ariso 荒磯 Rocky Shore

The Element

Ariso is a contraction of the word *araiso*, literally, rough seacoast, and is no longer used in modern Japanese. *Araiso* (荒磯), in turn, derives from other words such as *ara-iso* (有石), a word that no longer exists that would literally translate as "to be rocky" and *ara-iso* (現石), that would translate as a "place where the rocks are exposed." A seashore that is not covered with soft sand beaches but rather is stony and hard, beaten by rough storm waves, is called an *araiso*. These can be found almost anywhere along the Japanese seacoast where a promontory of land reaches out into the water. Unprotected, the waves scour the sand and soil off the surface of the beach, leaving the rough, stony bedrock to show.

In Gardens

The *Sakuteiki* specifically mentions the *ariso*, translated as rocky shore, as a motif for garden design. "In order to make the Ocean Style," the book suggests, "one must first re-create the image of a Rocky Shore. To do so, set stones as if they are heading out from the point of a wave-washed shore. Add many prominent stones with sharp edges at the shoreline, and a few Solitary Stones jutting out here and there. All these stones should appear dug out and exposed, as if they had been lashed by violent waves."[30] This passage, which encourages the reader to create a rocky shore, is followed later in the *Sakuteiki* by a contradictory passage that states, "Rocky shores are interesting to look at but, since they eventually fall into desolation, they should not be used as models for gardening."[31]

Archeological digs, too, provide clear examples of *ariso*. Unlike plants, which decompose over time, stones remain and give researchers some of the best evidence of how gardens were designed. The stones used along the edges of ponds, for instance, in some cases are preserved under thick layers of soil in exactly the same layout as they were centuries before. The garden at Mōtsūji Temple in Iwate Prefecture has an example of a rocky shore arrangement of stones along the edge of its partially extant, partially refurbished pond. Another example is an exhumed and restored garden in Nara City, from the Nara period (710–784), known as Tōin Teien, the Garden of the Eastern Hall.

The *Sakuteiki* also mentions a style of island design that incorporates an *ariso*, called the *isojima*, or rocky shore isle. It reads, "The Rocky Shore Style island is made by setting tall stones here and there. Following the 'request' of the stones, set them out on the shoreline roughly, boldly, and plant pine trees in between them. The trees need not be too tall, but they should be old, splendid in form, and laden with deep green needles."[32] The text suggests that the edge of the central island in a pond should be aligned with the center of the main hall of the property. A good example of this design — in which an island has an arrangement of stones in an *ariso* style on one side which is aligned with the center of the main hall — can be found at Jōruriji Temple is southern Kyōto Prefecture.

In Poetry

In poems, *ariso* was often used in combination with other words such as *ariso no umi* (rough seas on the rocky shore), *ariso no hama* (rocky shore of the beach), and *ariso no oki* (open seas off the rocky coast). As a *makura-kotoba*, *ariso* links to the word *ari*, meaning "to have." Also, the word *ura* meaning "bay" or "inlet" is an often-used poetic *engo* linked to *ariso*.

Perhaps more important than the specific allegory in this case is the general feeling, or *fuzei*, that the word *ariso* brought to the reader's mind. A rough and battered seacoast, lonely and distant, was a melancholy place, one of turmoil and hardship, a beautiful symbol for sadness and inner strife.

後撰和歌集　1298
　　題志らず
　　ひとしき子のみこ

我も思ふ　人も忘るな　ありそ海の　浦吹風の　止む時もなく
ware mo omou　hito mo wasuruna　ariso umi no　ura fuku kaze no　yamu toki mo naku
[first and third *ku* each have an additional syllable: *ji-amari*]

　　Gosen Wakashū 1298

　　Untitled
　　Hitoshikiko no Miko (Princess Kinshi Naishinnō)

Like the wind and waves
　　that gale relentlessly
　　　　against this rocky ocean beach
I think of you constantly
　　Don't forsake me

拾遺和歌集　631
　　よみ人知らず

かくてのみ　ありその浦の　浜千鳥　よそになきつゝ　恋ひやわたらむ
kakute nomi　ariso no ura no　hamachidori　yoso ni nakitsutsu　koi ya wataramu

　　Shūi Wakashū 631

　　Anonymous

Will I always be like this
　　a beach plover flying　distant
　　　　across the rock-strewn bay
　　crying over and over
　　　　forever in love

Asagao 朝顔 Morning Glory

The *kanji* used to write *asagao* has the literal meaning of "morning face." In modern Japanese *asagao* refers to a perennial vine called the Japanese morning glory (Ipomoea nil, Pharbitis nil). The plant referred to as *asagao* during the Heian period may have been this same vine, or it could also have been another plant. The two most likely possibilities are *kikyō*, the balloon flower or bell flower (Platycodon grandiflorum) and *mukuge*, the rose of Sharon (Hibiscus syriacus).

Asagao is mentioned in early writings as being one of the Seven Flowers of Autumn. Poem 1537 of the Nara-period anthology, the *Man'yōshū*, states that in autumn meadows there are seven flowers of note, and poem 1538, both by the same author, Yamanoue no Okura, lists those seven plants as being *hagi*, *obana* (*susuki*), *kuzu*, *nadeshiko*, *ominaeshi*, *fujibakama*, and *asagao*.[33] The modern list of seven autumn flowers is identical except that *asagao* has been replaced by *kikyō*, leading to the assumption that the name of the ancient *asagao* changed to *kikyō* at some point in history. It could also mean, however, that at some point one of the plants included in the list changed and the Heian-period *asagao* was not the modern *kikyō*. Although many modern texts concur that the Heian-period *asagao* was most likely the modern *kikyō*, the other two main possibilities, *mukuge* and modern-day *asagao*, seem better choices for three reasons.

First, Sei Shōnagon mentions in *Makura no Sōshi* that the *asagao* and the *yūgao* (literally, "evening face") resemble each other. *Yūgao*, bottle gourd (Lagenaria siceraria var. hispida), is known for its large fruit, which Sei Shōnagon finds hideous.[34] The flowers of the *yūgao* and those of the *mukuge* are reasonably similar. Perhaps not to a botanist but to a lay observer, their five-petalled crinkly-edged shape and typically white color would seem remarkably alike. And, very unlike the four-petalled, clean-edged *kikyō*. The flower of the modern-day *asagao* is also not unlike the *yūgao* — certainly closer than that of the *kikyō*. Second, in the passage in which Sei Shōnagon mentions that *yūgao* and *asagao* look alike, she also mentions *kikyō*. Since she mentions both *asagao* and *kikyō* in the same passage, it is most likely she is talking about two separate plants rather than using two names for the same plant. And, third, the *asagao* is often referred to as an ephemeral flower. Both the modern-day *asagao* and the *mukuge* flowers are known to last only a single day, while the *kikyō* flower is not so short-lived.

The flower of the *mukuge* is the closest to the descriptions and makes it seem a likely choice for the Heian-period *asagao*. That said, poems like number 114 from the *Shika Wakashū*, which describe *asagao* as being "suspended" or "leaning on" (*kakaru*, 懸かる) an open weave fence, make it sound just like the modern-day *asagao*, a light-stemmed vine that likes to wind its way up lattices. The long and short of it is, no one knows for certain which plant the Heian-period *asagao* really was.

In Gardens

There are several scenes in *Genji Monogatari* in which *asagao* appears in the garden. In the Yūgao chapter, a page boy walks among the flowers in the garden and plucks an *asagao* for Genji[35] and, in the Yadorigi chapter, Kaoru (Genji's purported son) picks a dew-covered *asagao*.[36] In both cases the flowers appear to have been planted in a part of the garden that was close to the residence, in a spot that was easily seen from inside the buildings and also easily approached by someone who had just stepped down off the veranda into the garden. This part of the garden was called the *senzai*, or near garden.

In Poetry

In poetry, the expression *asagao no* was used as a *makura-kotoba* linking to various words, the most prevalent of which was *hakanashi* or transient. The impermanence of all earthly things and the ephemeral quality of existence appear as underlying or overt themes time and time again in Heian-period literature and poetry. One commonly used symbol of evanescence was dew, which is at times depicted in combination with *asagao*, as in the previous passage from *Genji Monogatari*. In some cases, the two are compared to each other as in the second passage below from the *Murasaki Shikibu Shū* in which the fleeting dew competes with the fading *asagao* flower.[37]

伊勢物語 37
　むかし、男、色好みなりける女にあへりけり。うしろめたくや思ひけむ。

われならで　下紐解くな　あさがほの　夕影またぬ　花にはありとも

ware narade　shitahimo toku na　asagao no　yūkage matanu　hana ni wa ari tomo

Ise Monogatari 37

 Long long ago, a man met a lusty woman
   who turned him to fretful thoughts.

So fickle and quick
 this *asagao* flower
it can't even wait for twilight
  don't be that way loosing your underbelts

   for other men than me

紫式部集　53
　世中のさはかしきころあさかほを人のもとへやるとて

きえぬ間の　身をはしるしる　朝顔の　露とあらそふ　世を歎く哉

kienu ma no　mi wo wa shirushiru　asagao no　tsuyu to arasou　yo wo nageku kana

Murasaki Shikibu Shū 53

 Upon sending an *asagao* flower to someone at a time
when the world was restless

 I know it all so well
  we're here then we're gone
    condemned to race
  the fleeting dew the fading flower
   what a sad, sad world this is

Ashi 葦 Reed Grass

Ashi, or reed grass (Phragmites communis), is a perennial reed that can be found growing along the seashore as well as on the banks of both ponds and rivers. A vigorous grower, it can reach 2 meters (6 feet) or more in height and cover extensive areas of low water by shorelines. These massive sweeps of grass are called *ashihara* or reed fields. The name is usually written with the character 葦 but 蘆, 葭, or 芦 can also be used. Nowadays the same plant is alternately called *yoshi* instead of *ashi* because the word *ashi* is a homonym for the word "bad" (悪し) whereas *yoshi* (良し) means "good."

Ashi has a central place within the ancient mythologies of Japan. The very first lines of the *Nihon Shoki, Chronicles of Japan*, which detail a Sino-Japanese genesis mythology of the world, relate how the primordial nothingness that existed before the world as we know it came into being separated into pure-bright parts and heavy-clouded parts, becoming heaven and earth, respectively. It continues to describe how land masses began floating about like fish on water and a reed-shoot, *ashi-kabi*, sprouted, becoming the god Kuni-toko-tachi-no Mikoto.[38] Also, one of the first primordial masses that developed following that, which according to this mythology became the land of Japan, was called the Reed-Plains, Ashihara, or the Central Land of Reed-Plains, Ashihara no Nakatsu Kuni.[39] So the image of *ashi* is inextricably linked to ancient mythologies.

In a more practical vein, *ashi* was also used for thatching roofs (and still is the favored material for thatch roofing) and for making simple fences, *ashi-gaki*. In this guise, it was a fundamental construction material that would have been very familiar to people during the Heian period. *Ashi* growing in the wild and in gardens, or being harvested and used for any number of purposes, would have been an everyday scene.

The *Sakuteiki* mentions *ashi* as one of the plants used to create the Wetland Style of gardening, *numa-ike no yō*, which was described as a little inlet planted with various water plants. The planting was supposed to be done densely so that only a glimpse of water would appear between the plants.[40]

The *Sakuteiki* also mentions a garden style called the Reed Style, *ashide no yō* (literally, reed-hand style). *Ashide* was a type of drawing that mixed painting and calligraphy depicting meandering, convoluted shorelines with clumps of grasses growing on the banks, or meadow scenes within which were fluidly-drawn and cleverly hidden calligraphy.

> In the Reed Style, hill-forms should not be too high. A few stones should be set along the edge of Meadows or on the water's edge; next to those, some grass-like plants such as grass bamboo or tall field-grasses should be planted. Plums, willows, or other such trees with soft and gentle forms can also be planted according to one's taste.[41]

In *Genji Monogatari*, the gist of an *ashide* painting is described as being the juxtaposition of the energy or strength of the lines that represent the rippling water's edge and the lively, ruffled, bristle-like appearance of the *ashi*, the former being horizontal and flowing and the latter being upright and linear. One can imagine it was this contrast of soft, flowing lines and strong upright strokes that was sought after in a garden design called a Reed Style.[42]

In *Makura no Sōshi*, Shōnagon describes *ashi* as having blossoms that are unremarkable — of course, the flowers of reeds and grasses are so understated we don't usually think of them as "flowers" in the ornamental sense. However, notes the author, since *ashi* reeds are incorporated into the streamers used at Shintō ceremonies, they must be special somehow. She particularly likes *ashi* when planted at the water's edge, which confirms what was written in the *Sakuteiki*.

As well as being planted in gardens, *ashi* stems were used to make rustic fences, *ashi-gaki*, that separated sections of the garden or acted as screens. In *Genji Monogatari*, these are mentioned from time to time including one often-painted scene, in the Tokonatsu chapter, in which a reed fence represents the barrier between two lovers.[43]

In Poetry

The word *ashi* could be used by itself in a poem or in combination with other words such as *ashibe* (reed banks, 葦辺), *ashihara* (reed fields, 葦原), *ashikari* (reed harvesting, 葦刈), *ashibi* (reed fire, 葦火), and *ashigaki* (reed fence, 葦垣). Mentioning *ashi* in a poem evokes images of the daily life of people living in rural areas, either gathering reeds or using reeds for making fences and mats and, as such, is a pastoral image. In a rural village, the reed harvest typically took place in late autumn after the rice harvest, so *ashi* also becomes a seasonal indicator — that of autumn. This, plus the fact that the image of the *ashi* is related to that of the seashore or water's edge also lends it an overtone of loneliness.

As a *makura-kotoba*, *ashi* links to words such as *furu*, meaning to become old, and *midaru*, which means "to be in disarray." The connection to *furu* stems from the fact that fences, roofs, and other things made of *ashi*, because it is not a terribly strong material, would become disheveled over the years if not repaired. The image of broken and forlorn reed fences or mossy, aged thatched roofs must have been common enough to have become a standard motif. The connection to *midaru*, to be in disarray, also derives from this image of aging as well as from the image of reeds being harvested. When these tall grasses are cut off at the base with a sickle, they fall every which way, scattering about in the most random fashion, thus evoking the image of disarray or of emotional unsettledness.

万葉集　919

若の浦に　潮満ち来れば　潟をなみ　葦辺をさして　鶴鳴き渡る
waka no ura ni　shio michi kureba　kata wo nami　ashibe wo sashite　tazu naki wataru

Man'yōshū 919

When high tide
　　　Comes flooding over the sand bars
　　　　　of Waka-no-ura Bay
Cranes lift wing and cry
　　　Arcing toward endless seas of reeds

山家集　220
　　西行

舟すゑし　みなとの蘆間　棹立てて　心ゆくらん　五月雨の頃
fune sueshi　minato no ashima　sao tatete　kokoro yukuran　samidare no koro

Sankashū 220
　　Saigyō

Having stopped his boat
　　　in the snug harbor among the reeds
　　　　　he plants his pole
A spot of peace at last, perhaps
　　　in these troubling summer rains

HAGI

oki akashi
mitsutsu nagamuru
hagi no ue no
tsuyu fuki midaru
aki no yo no kaze

Goshūi Wakashū 295

BUSH CLOVER

Staying up all night
watching sadly over the
swaying bush clover
Its dew scattered to the night
by the autumn wind

おきあかし見つゝながむる

萩がうへの露ふきみだる

秋の夜の風

Ayame あやめ Sweet Rush

Ayame, sweet rush or sweet flag (Acorus calamus), is a perennial herbaceous plant that grows in the shallows along the edges of lakes and ponds. Due to historical changes, the name of this plant always causes a bit of confusion. In the Heian period, Acorus calamus was called *ayame* while in modern Japanese it is called *shōbu*. An aquatic plant with a non-ornamental flower, Acorus calamus is, as mentioned, called sweet rush or sweet flag in English. The plant that is called *ayame* nowadays is an iris with a showy flower — purple, white, or a patterned mixture thereof — that is called Japanese iris or blood iris in English (Iris sanguinea). As if things didn't need to be more convoluted, another plant with a similar name, which is planted extensively in every large park in Japan, is the *hana-shōbu*, Japanese water iris (Iris ensata). To make things clear, the Heian-period *ayame* was an aquatic rush — not an iris — about 60 cm (2 feet) high with flat, blade-like leaves that are somewhat aromatic, and a stubby, non-descript flower pod (spadix).

Acorus calamus is known in various cultures throughout the word as a medicinal plant primarily for its root. The rhizome is considered a general stimulant, an aphrodisiac in particular (an idea exacerbated, perhaps, by the phallic-shaped flower pod), and a hallucinogen in large doses. Whether Heian-period custom included psychoactive uses of the root is not recorded, but the root was subject of a contest in which contestants brought samples and vied for the longest. The leaves of the *yomogi* plant (Mugwort or Moxa, Artemisia princeps) and those of the *ayame* were believed to be effective in warding off evil spirits and both were used during the *tango no sechie* festival on the 5th day of the 5th month. In *Makura no Sōshi*, Sei Shōnagon describes how people decorate their clothes with sweet smelling *ayame* (and *yomogi*), or the long roots of the *ayame*, and parade about the streets of the capital.[44] She reiterates later on how sweet smelling *ayame* is, even after having lasted through the autumn and winter and looking pale and withered. After the shift in society during the Kamakura period (1185–1333) to the social dominance of the military families, the *tango no sechie* festival took on the overtones of being a blessing for boys, and the blade-like leaf of the *ayame* was noted because it is reminiscent of a sword.

In Gardens

The *Sakuteiki* mentions *ayame* as one of the plants used to create the Wetland Style of gardening, *numa-ike no yō* (see *ashi*).[45] In *Genji Monogatari*, when the Prince builds a great four-section garden at his Rokujō palace, with each directional quarter of the garden devoted to a different season, he plants *ayame* in the southeast section — the spring garden — as a marker for the Festival of the 5th Month, *tango no sechie*.[46] *Ayame* shows up time and again in the *Makura no Sōshi*, often alongside the *yomogi* and often in association with the *tango no sechie*.

In Poetry

In poetry *ayame* is, of course, a seasonal indicator strongly related to the 5th month, which corresponded more to June than to May. Its relation to the *tango no sechie* festival and its use as a medicinal plant give the *ayame* interesting overtones — not a plant of physical beauty but one of mysterious curative powers. Being linked with the 5th month, it is often coupled with the cuckoo bird, *hototogisu*, which is also used as a poetic symbol of the 5th month.

As a pillow word, usually in the form *ayamegusa* — which simply means *ayame*-grass — *ayame* is linked to several other words. One is *nagaki* meaning long, most likely a reference to the root. Another is *ne*, which can mean root but can also mean sleep, as in sleeping with a lover. A third is *ayame mo shiranu*, as in the following poem. In this case *ayame* means pattern of woven cloth and the expression *ayame mo shiranu* means "cannot discern the pattern" or more figuratively, "can't distinguish between" or "is blind to."

古今和歌集　469
　　よみ人知らず

郭公　なくや五月の　あやめぐさ　あやめも知らぬ　恋もするかな
hototogisu　naku ya satsuki no　ayamegusa　ayame mo shiranu　koi mo suru kana

Kokin Wakashū 469

Anonymous

Sad cuckoo
　　crying over the sweet rush
　　　　in the rainy month of June
The pattern beyond comprehension
　　my love is but blind

千載和歌集　168
　　前中納言雅頼
　　久我内大臣の家にて旅宿菖蒲といへる心をよめる

都こ人　引きなつくしそ　あやめ草　かりねの床の　枕ばかりは
miyakobito　hiki na tsukushi so　ayamegusa　karine no toko no　makura bakari wa

Senzai Wakashū 168
　　Former Vice Council of State Masayori
　　Written in the spirit of the sweet rush seen when staying
at the house of Kuga, Minister of the Interior

All you folks from the Capital
　　don't yank out all the sweet rush
　　　　right down to the roots
At least leave a pillow's worth
　　for this poor traveler's bed

Fuji 藤 *Wisteria*

Fuji, the Japanese wisteria, is a plant well-known to gardeners around the world. The wisteria that was used in Heian-period gardens, and referred to in the poems, was most likely Wisteria floribunda, although another possibility is the less profusely-blooming "wild cousin," known today as *yamafuji*, Wisteria brachybotyrs, the silky wisteria. The wisteria is a powerful vine that grows up trees in the wild, setting cascades of lavender-colored blooms, called racemes, in April and May. Floribunda winds itself in a clock-wise fashion and its racemes open progressively from top to bottom, while brachybotyrs winds counter clock-wise and sets its flowers all at once.

In Gardens

There is ample evidence of *fuji* being used in Heian-period gardens. Archeological digs at Heian-period residential sites have turned up remains of *fuji* seed pods[47] and literature provides many, many references. In *Genji Monogatari*, one remarkable scene involving *fuji* in a garden takes place in the chapter aptly named Fuji no Uraba, New Wisteria Leaves.[48] It is the 4th month, the wisteria is in outstandingly good form, blooming profusely in the garden of the Minister of the Interior. Seeing the blooms he arranges for music to be played to add to the atmosphere. That evening, he decides he will at long last offer his daughter's hand in marriage to young Yūgiri, Prince Genji's son. He writes a poem about the wisteria, ties a beautiful bloom to it, and sends it to Yūgiri along with an invitation to come that night. Yūgiri arrives, shares a drink with his host, and is offered his daughter as a bride. As the guest and host talk back and forth, however, they do not express all their thoughts in so many words. Rather, they express them in poems that they invent on the spot and sing back and forth, all of which use *fuji* as a metaphor for what they intend to convey. Nowhere is the relationship between poetry and garden made more clear than here, where elements within the garden act as inspiration for the impromptu creation of poems.

One interesting aspect of the wisteria in the Minister's garden is that it was not growing on an arbor, as is typical these days. Wisteria is an aggressive climber and is often considered an invasive species if not controlled, for instance by limiting its growth to a fixed structure like a trellis or arbor. In the Minister's garden, the wisteria is allowed to grow up a pine tree. The contrast of the dark evergreen needles and the bright lavender blooms made for an especially pleasing sight. In *Makura no Sōshi*, Sei Shōnagon writes that the long tassel of blooms that the wisteria puts out is among the things she considers to be splendid, *medetaki mono*.[49]

One of the main characters in *Genji Monogatari* is a woman who is referred to as Fujitsubo. *Fuji*, of course, means wisteria, and *tsubo* refers to one of the inner courtyards of the palace. The gardens in these *tsubo* usually featured a prominent plant after which the court was named, thus Fujitsubo was the Wisteria Court. Court ladies whose apartments faced onto a certain court were referred to by the name of the court, thus Fujitusbo was both the informal name of the courtyard and the princess who lived next to it.

In Poetry

The blooms the wisteria sets are so profuse that the plant is often expressed in poetry as *fuji-nami* (藤波), wisteria-waves, or *fuji-goromo* (藤衣), wisteria-robes. The vigor of the vine, the masses of flowers, and the springtime connection make it a perfect image for poems of passionate love. Wisteria was also used as a metaphor for the powerful Fujiwara family simply because it is the first character of their name. The Fujiwara were courtiers who became so complexly inter-married with the imperial family that, by the end of the Heian period, they had essentially usurped control of the court. In poems that use *fuji* to mean Fujiwara, a linked image of a pine often shows up. In this case the strong, evergreen pine is the imperial household upon which the wisteria rests for support.

Fuji can also be linked in poems to the word *fuchi* (淵), because of the similar sound of the words. *Fuchi* means a deep pool of water, and poems that use these words in combination often mention the reflection of wisteria blooms on the surface of the water.

万葉集　1901

藤波の　咲く春の野に　延ふ葛の　下よし恋ひば　久しくもあらむ

fuji nami no　sakeru haru no ni　hau kuzu no　shita yo shi koi ba　hisashiku mo aramu

Man'yōshū 1901

Some love like
　　waves of wisteria blossoms above the Spring meadow
　　　　　me　　I'm like low-growing kudzu
Hiding my love
　　this is going to take forever

詞花和歌集　257
　　俊子内親王大進
　　久しく音せぬ男につかはしける

とはぬまを　うらむらさきに　さく藤の　何とてまつに　かゝりそめけむ

towanu ma wo　uramurasaki ni　saku fuji no　nani tote matsu ni　kakarisomekemu

Shika Wakashū 257
　　Princess Shunshi's third-rank lady in waiting
　　A poem sent to a man who has long not written

For so long I have heard nothing
　　I flower　　a deep-lavender wisteria
　　　　yet am resentful, bitter
Why on earth did I cling
　　to that pine of mine

Hagi 萩 Bush Clover

The Element

Hagi is known as bush clover in English. It is a large shrub of the Pea family, growing up to 2 meters (6.5 feet) in height and breadth. It has long pendulous stems that cascade out in all directions from the center. This form produces a waterfall-like effect when in full bloom. There are many varieties of *hagi* but the two most likely to have been planted in Heian-period gardens, and written about in the poetry of that time, are Lespedeza bicolor and Lespedeza thunbergii. In Japan today, the former is called *yama-hagi* and the latter is *miyagino-hagi*. Bush clover grows throughout Japan and, in the Heian period when meadows were common around the capital, bush clover became a plant associated with meadow landscapes. It was thought of fondly by the people of the Heian court, enough so that they would attach sprays of flowering bush clover to letters they sent. Sei Shōnagon mentions a letter attached to a spray of *hagi* that was still wet with dew and fragrant.[50]

In Gardens

It is clear from the many, many references in literature that bush clover was planted in the gardens of the Heian period. One interesting insight comes from a passage in the Azumaya chapter of *Genji Monogatari* in which it is remarked that a certain person (Niou, a grandson of Genji) has bush clover that has a particularly beautiful appearance and the writer wonders *where he got the seeds*.[51] Little is known of how gardens were planted but most evidence points toward transplanting. An entry from 1012, for instance, in *Midō Kanpakuki* (the diary of Regent Fujiwara

Michinaga), states that: "…people of the house have left for Saga to collect plants." "Collecting plants" was referred to as *senzai wo horu*.[52] Yet here, in *Genji Monogatari*, we find a suggestion that at least some plants were planted in gardens as seeds.

Still, transplanting was most likely. Sei Shōnagon expresses her annoyance (she's often annoyed with things) when she finds, upon going to look at a favorite bush clover she had planted in the garden, someone nonchalantly digging it up and walking away with it. In any case, she does use the word "planted" so we know that bush clovers were both planted and seeded in gardens.[53]

The branches of the bush clover are, as mentioned, supple and pendulous. When the shrub is wetted down with morning dew, the branches droop even further, giving the form a sadness that appealed to the Heian period writers. In *Makura no Sōshi*, Sei Shōnagon mentions the *hagi* flowers in deep hues and the branches as willowy and graceful. When wet by morning dew it is particularly graceful, she says, and later she mentions how beautiful it is to watch the branches spring back up when the sun dries the dew.[54]

In Poetry

The bush clover is one of the most-mentioned plants in early Japanese poetry. In the *Man'yōshū*, there are over 140 poems that include *hagi*, more than any other plant. This is in part because of the aforementioned sadness inherent in the drooping form of the shrub, and the way it catches dew in such a beautiful way. It is also because it flowers in autumn, when little else does, and thus draws attention to itself. The *kanji* for *hagi* (萩) was not used frequently until the middle of the Heian period. It used to be applied to another plant, the *kawara yomogi* (河原蓬, Artemisia capillaries), but because the character incorporates the radical for grass (艹) and the character for autumn (秋), and since *hagi* became the "autumn grass," the *kanji* was reapplied to the bush clover. Needless to say, the first poetic quality associated with *hagi* is its association with autumn.

In poems, *hagi* is used as a *makura-kotoba* linking to words such as *shinai/shinayaka* (flexible or supple), *utsuru* (to change or shift, such as the changing seasons), and *hanano* (a field of flowers). *Hagi* also often appears with male deer (whose baying is always mournful), or with dew, as we saw before, or with both deer and dew as in the poem below. The stag is an image of forlorn love, the sad *hagi* is the object of that love. Sei Shōnagon mentions that she has heard that the stag is known to stand by the bush clover and this touches her heart.[55]

Hagi is also associated with wind, in particular the cold winds of autumn. The image of the bush clover being flung about in the wind is indicative of the inner turmoil that the poem's author wishes to convey. In a chapter of *Genji Monogatari*, appropriately named Nowaki, Autumn Winds, there is a scene that captures this feeling in which the winds strip all the dew from the bush clover branches.

万葉集　1598
　　大伴宿祢家持秋歌三首

さ雄鹿の　朝立つ野辺の　秋萩に　玉と見るまで　置ける白露
saoshika no　asa tatsu nobe no　akihagi ni　tama to miru made　okeru shiratsuyu

Man'yōshū 1598

One of three poems by Ōtomo no Yakamochi about autumn

The lonely buck

pauses in the early morning meadow

by the autumn bush clover

laden with glistening dew until it

sparkles like cascades of jewels

後拾遺和歌集　295
　　伊勢大輔
　　物思ふ事有ける頃萩を見て詠める

起きあかし　見つゝながむる　萩の上の　露吹きみだる　秋の夜の風
oki akashi　mitsutsu nagamuru　hagi no ue no　tsuyu fuki midaru　aki no yo no kaze

Goshūi Wakashū 295

Ise no Ōsuke

Composed upon seeing *hagi* at a time when I had

thoughts on my mind

Staying up all night

watching sadly over the

swaying bush clover

Its dew scattered to the night

by the autumn wind

Hashi 橋 Bridge

There are several words that are pronounced *hashi*. One is "bridge," which is the focus of this section, but in fact the word *hashi* has a more basic meaning of "an edge" and anything that crosses the divide between two edges is also called a *hashi*. A bridge, which crosses between two banks of a river or two cliff-faces of a ravine, is an obvious example of something that crosses between two edges. Stairs, which are called *kaidan* nowadays, were called *hashi* in the Heian period.

The passages describing the creation of the lands of Japan given in the *Nihon Shoki, Chronicles of Japan*, and the *Kojiki, Records of Ancient Matters*, mention two gods standing on the Floating Bridge of Heaven, *ama no uki hashi*, and stirring with a spear into the primordial soup beneath them caused the first incipient island to congeal.[56] This bridge was perceived as a link between the heavenly world of divine beings and the physical world of the earth, and is one of many ways in which bridges were seen as links between "this word" and "other worlds."

By the time of the Heian period, there were many kinds of bridges that were being built including stone bridges (*iwa hashi*), floating bridges (*uki hashi*), simple plank bridges (*uchi hashi* and *tsugi hashi*), suspended bridges (*kake hashi* and *tsuri hashi*), and Chinese style bridges (*kara hashi* and *sori hashi*).

In Gardens

We know that bridges were used in gardens from ancient times. The first record, for instance, of a gardener in Japan is in the *Nihon Shoki, Chronicles of Japan*, in the year 612, which mentions a man from the Korean kingdom of Paekche with the skills of "making mountains" — in other words making hill forms in gardens — who came to Japan to seek his way. It is recorded that he ended up making the form of Mount Sumeru and a Chinese-style bridge in the Southern Garden of the Empress Suiko.[57]

We know from several sources that bridges were used in Heian-period gardens: literature, such as the *Sakuteiki, Murasaki Shikibu Nikki,* and *Genji Monogatari*; paintings of gardens (although the oldest of these is from the following Kamakura period (1185–1333); and archeological evidence which has located remains of the bridge piers, though not the bridges themselves, which were wooden and have since decomposed. Many Heian-period gardens featured an irregularly-shaped pond of some size, large or small, in the center of the southern garden. Within the pond were islands, some of which were connected to land by bridges. Paintings show some of these bridges to be flat and some arched, the latter being called *sori hashi*, a term that shows up in both the *Sakuteiki* and *Genji Monogatari*. The *Sakuteiki* is rather specific about how the *sori hashi* should be placed, aligned so that the underside of its curve would not be revealed to people sitting within the residence. The bridge was also, ideally, supposed to be located slightly off-center from the main hall of the property.[58] *Murasaki Shikibu Nikki* mentions a *kara hashi,* or Chinese-style bridge, undoubtedly wooden, perhaps curved, usually with posts and railings that were painted a vermillion color.[59]

In the *Murasaki Shikibu Nikki* and *Genji Monogatari*, the word *hashi* is used to mean a bridge in the garden and also in reference to the bridges that were part of the system of roofed corridors, known as *wata-dono* or *watari-dono*, that connected one hall of the residence to another. These bridges might also be called *sori hashi*, if they were curved, or *uchi hashi*, presumably if they were unroofed, temporarily-built structures. *Uchi hashi* usually refers to a plank bridge set up for temporary use like scaffolding.

In Poetry

In poetry, the word *hashi* is often used as an *uta-makura* — a symbol of a certain location — by mentioning the name of a famous bridge that has a particular story connected to it or its locality. One such example is the reference to the bridge over the Uji River and the goddess that acts as a protector of that bridge, *Uji no hashi-hime*, which translates literally as Princess of the Uji Bridge. Another example relates back to an ancient story of the Asuka period (538–710) about the building of the Nagara no hashi bridge and how the construction required the sacrifice of a human to be buried along with the piers of the bridge.

Hashi can also have many symbolic meanings. As one might expect, the theme of bridges as connectors between separate worlds shows up, as do the themes of passage, crossing, and traveling. Bridges were often torn from their moorings and washed away in storms so they became an image of impermanence and were used to evoke the sentiments of sadness and ephemerality. This is revealed nowhere more clearly than in the word *tae*, meaning extinguished, which is considered to be an *engo*, or associative word, related to *hashi*. The image of remnant piers of old bridges — the aftermath of such destruction — is placed in poems for this reason. Another poetic connection related to *hashi* comes in the form of the word *uki hashi*, which can mean either floating bridge (浮き橋) or, written another way, can mean a moment of gloom or despair (憂き端). That double meaning lends an added sense of pathos to a poem that uses the expression *uki hashi*.

Tsugi hashi is the name given to a simple bridge made by setting wooden planks from sand bar to sand bar across a shallow river or inlet. The shifting nature of the landscape they were built in meant they were often temporary, soon to be washed away. The zig-zag path they formed appeared haphazard and, by its very nature, was at once broken into sections and also connected. In poems, the word *tsugi hashi* could thus be related to images of ephemerality, irregularity, and being connected yet separate.

One final note. Since the word *fumi* can be both a conjugated form of the verb *fumu*, meaning "to step upon," and the noun meaning "a letter" (as in a letter written to another person), some poems use this as a *kake-kotoba* that links the images of stepping on and crossing a bridge with that of the receipt of, or the sending of, a letter.

後撰和歌集　1122
　　四條御息所の女
　　男の女の文を隠しけるを見てもとの妻（め）の書きつけ侍りける

へだてける　人の心の　うき橋を　あやうきまでも　ふみみつる哉
hedatekeru　hito no kokoro no　ukihashi wo　ayauki made mo　fumi mitsuru kana

> *Gosen Wakashū* 1122
> 　　Shijō miyasundokoro no musume
> 　　Jotted down by a woman who found a letter from
> another woman that her man had hidden
>
> The rickety floating bridge
> 　　that leads so far away
> 　　　　to your heart
> Ever-shifting and treacherous —
> 　　I step along it as I read

千載和歌集　1165
　　源俊頼朝臣

かきたえし　真間の継橋　ふみみれば　隔てたる　霞も晴れて　向かへるがごと
kakitaeshi　mama no tsugihashi　fumi mireba　hedatetaru　kasumi mo harete　mukaeru ga goto

> *Senzai Wakashū* 1165
> 　　Minamoto no Toshiyori no Ason[60]
>
> My letters broke off　　yes
> 　　but just seeing yours
> 　　　　and it's as if I'm stepping across
> the plank bridges at the Mama inlet
> 　　The mists of distance lift
> 　　　　and we meet — together once more

Hasu 蓮 Lotus

Lotuses are aquatic plants with large, circular leaves and large ornamental flowers. The plant is also called the Sacred Lotus because of its association with various Asian religions, including Hinduism and Buddhism. The botanical name of the species commonly found in Japan is Nelumbo nucifera. The lotus plant sets its roots in the muddy bottoms of ponds, and sends stalks up toward the light. The first leaves float on the surface of the water, leaves that unfold later in the season rise up above the water surface, and the flowers rise even further above those. This attribute of leaves and flowers being held aloft, not floating, is one of the major differences between lotuses and water lilies, with which they are often confused.

Lotuses were probably brought from mainland Asia to Japan at least some 2,000 years ago along with other agricultural plants such as rice. Throughout eastern Asia, lotuses have appeared in religious imagery, including Buddhism, the teachings of which were brought to Japan in the 6th century. Lotuses are mentioned in the *Nihon Shoki, Chronicles of Japan*, to be growing in the Bay of Kusaka, which means they were naturalized by the early 7th century.[61] Many parts of the lotus are edible including the young stems, the seeds, and the roots, the last of which can grow to become large chambered tubers.

In Gardens

Ponds were central features in gardens from well before the Heian period and lotuses could grow easily in their warm shallow waters. Sei Shōnagon, in *Makura no Sōshi*, mentions a visit to the palace of His Excellency, the Major Captain of the Smaller Palace of the First Ward, a residence called Ko-shirakawa, or Lesser White River. It is summer and terribly hot. The

High Nobles were performing a ceremony and people from all over were crowding their carriages in to see. The only respite from the heat, she writes, was to look at the lotuses in the pond.[62] In the Maboroshi chapter of *Genji Monogatari*, too, we find Prince Genji in a cool spot looking out at the lotuses for respite from the summer heat.[63]

Again in *Makura no Sōshi* Sei Shōnagon writes in a section on various plants that lotuses look so fine floating on the still, clear water of a pond, their many large and small leaves making a splendid sight indeed. It is wonderful, she says, to take a leaf and press it against something (to make an imprint).[64] She also mentions how, if you pick up tiny lotus leaves that are floating on a pond and look at them they are so adorable.[65]

Lotus leaves are large and round, slightly cupped and somewhat drum-like. If you tap on them, they make a dull report. In a short section on "Things that are Pleasant," *kokochi yoge naru mono*, Sei Shōnagon mentions how lovely it is to hear the pitter-patter of a passing shower on the leaves.[66]

In Poetry

In Buddhism, the lotus is seen as representing nobility and purity. Its roots grow in the muddy bottom of shallow ponds and lake shores. Its leaves, however, rise above the surface of the muddy waters, and its flower rises further still, producing a singularly exquisite bloom. This was incorporated into Buddhist teachings as a parable for personal religious development — the capability of humans to rise above their "murky roots" in the material world to the realm of spiritual enlightenment.

The lotus is often linked to the deity Amida Buddha, or Amida Nyorai in Japanese (Amitâbha in Sanskrit). The heavenly realm of Amida is known as the Western Paradise, Saihō Gokuraku Jōdo. In paintings, it is represented as a land far across a great ocean, like an island in the sea. Amida's palace sits in the center and in front of the palace spreads a pond filled with blooming lotuses.

The first leaves that appear in spring float on the surface of the water like water lily leaves. After that, however, the leaves rise above the water on sturdy stalks and are held aloft. In some ponds there are so many lotuses the surface of the water disappears beneath a sea of huge upturned leaves. These large leaves are somewhat cup-shaped, and when it rains, water collects in the hollow of the leaf. The combination of a waxy composition and a covering of microscopic hairs on the leaf causes that water to ball up into jewel-like beads. When these beads of water grow too heavy for the stalk, the leaf nods, the water slides with a slurp into the pond, and the leaf begins to fill again. These "jewels" are mentioned in poems used in the introductory lines of this book in which Prince Genji and his love Murasaki no Ue gaze upon lotuses in the garden, and the jewels of dew on them, and spontaneously create poems.

With the connection to Amida's Pure Land, the image of the lotus is not only connected with purity, but with the afterlife. In the passage between Genji and Murasaki, the nearness of her death brought thoughts of the brevity of life — no longer than dew on leaves. Similarly, in the second poem that follows, "awaiting the flowering of the lotus," can be seen as awaiting Buddhist enlightenment, whether it be enlightened awareness in this life, or permanent enlightenment as rebirth in Nirvana.

古今和歌集　165
　　はちすのつゆを見てよめる

蓮葉の　濁りに染まぬ　心もて　なにかは露を　玉とあざむく
hachisuba no　nigori ni shimanu　kokoro mote　nanika wa tsuyu wo　tama to azamuku

Kokin Wakashū 165
　　Written upon seeing dew on lotus

Noble lotus
　　even muddy waters can't stain
　　　　such a pure heart
Why then these deceits
　　conjuring jewels from dew-drops

山家集　1237
　　西行

波のたつ　心の水を　しづめつつ　咲かむ蓮を　今は待つかな
nami no tatsu　kokoro no mizu wo　shizumetsutsu　sakamu hachisu wo　ima wa matsu kana

Sankashū 1237
　　Saigyō

I have stilled
　　the waves roiling
　　　　in the waters of my heart
And now await
　　the flowering of the lotus

Hinoki 檜 桧 Japanese Cypress

The Element

Hinoki, the Japanese cypress (Chamaecyparis obtusa), is a 30 to 50 meter (100 to 165 feet) tall coniferous evergreen tree that grows in thick forests throughout Japan. Today's forests are more often than not dense plantations of harvestable stock, but the poems of the ancient past tell us that, at least in some places, the mountains were naturally thickly covered with these trees. The name, *hi no ki*, is thought to have the original meaning of "tree of fire" because sticks of the sap-rich wood, when rubbed together, were used to start fires. A large, straight-growing tree, with a straight grain and resin that makes it rot resistant, *hinoki* has been a favored material for building palaces, shrines, and temples since ancient times. The *Nihon Shoki, Chronicles of Japan*, even mentions it as the appropriate wood for this purpose.[67]

At times *hinoki* is referred to as *maki* (真木, 眞木), which means "true/genuine tree" and can be used to refer to high quality specimens of either *sugi* (Cryptomeria japonica) or *hinoki*. *Hinoki* wood was also used to make other fine objects such as fences (*higaki*), which were woven from thin slats of the wood, and boxes for food (*hiwarigo*). The bark (*hiwada*) was used to make roofing shingles.

In Gardens

Archeological evidence points to the use of *hinoki* in Heian-period gardens. Specifically, *hinoki* seed cones have been found at Heian-period sites. The *Sakuteiki*, too, mentions the use of *hinoki* in the garden. The tree appears only once but with a special purpose. Each of the cardinal directions was believed to be inhabited by one of the Four Guardian Gods (*shijin*) and was symbolized and enhanced by a landscape feature: flowing water in the east, a pond in the south, a large pathway in the west, and a hill in the north. If the northern hill was not naturally present or possible to create, it could, according to the *Sakuteiki*, be replaced by three cypress trees.[68]

Sei Shōnagon, in *Makura no Sōshi*, describes the *hinoki* as being a tree one does not see often, implying it was not common in urban gardens, but that in the 5th month, the sound of wind flowing through its needles sounds just like rain.[69] She also mentions that she likes the sight of snow that has fallen on a roof made of *hinoki* shingles and the sound of rain and hail as it falls on wooden roof boards, maybe something like those in the poem that follows.[70]

In Poetry

In poetry, *hinoki* is linked to wood as a construction material and to images of the deep mountains. Expressions such as *maki saku*, to split *hinoki*, and *maki tsumu*, to gather *hinoki* logs, are examples of the former. Examples of the latter would be the term *hibara*, a thick forest[71] of *hinoki* trees, and its use alongside certain poetic words: *okuyama* (deep mountains), *kasumi* (mist), *kiri* (fog), *ame* (rain), and *yuki* (snow). All of these images layered together give the sense of a mysterious place, deep in the forested mountains, a quality that is now referred to as *shinzan yūkoku*, "deep mountains mysterious valleys."

拾遺和歌集　816
　　よみ人志らず

巻向の　檜原の霞　立返り　かくこそは見め　飽かぬ君哉
makimoku no　hibara no kasumi　tachikaeri　kaku koso wa mime　akanu kimi kana

　　Shūi Wakashū 816
　　Anonymous

　　Pale mists lift
　　　　through the cypress forests of Makimoku
　　　　　　returning as I would to you
　　to look on you so tenderly
　　　　my heart unwavering

千載和歌集　444
　　左近中將良經
　　閑居聞霰といへる心をよみ侍りける

さゆる夜の　まきのいたやの　ひとりねに　心くだけと　あられふるなり
sayuru yo no　maki no itaya no　hitorine ni　kokoro kudake to　arare furu nari

　　Senzai Wakashū 444
　　Fujiwara no Yoshitsune
　　Written on the theme of the sound of hail in a quiet and
secluded place

　　A frigid night
　　　　in my simple wood-board home
　　　　　　finds me lying low and lonely
　　The relentless pattering of hail
　　　　falling　　urging my heart to break

Hotaru 蛍 Firefly

The Element

Hotaru, fireflies, need no introduction; similar insects are found in many places around the world. The two most common fireflies in Japan, and the ones most likely referred to in Heian period literature, are the *Genji-botaru* (Luciola cruciata) and the *Heike-botaru* (Luciola lateralis). The habitats of both include grassy meadows and streams. Of course, the firefly is known for is ability to produce a pale-green, flashing light from organs in the lower abdomen due to a chemical reaction called bioluminescence.

The *Utsuho Monogatari* (late 10th century), contains a passage in which the Emperor, wanting to steal a glance at a certain woman in the middle of the night, has a retainer collect many fireflies that he puts in the sleeve of his robe. The summer-weight, gossamer fabric lets their light through and he uses his sleeve as a gentle flashlight.[72] Similarly, in the chapter aptly named Hotaru of *Genji Monogatari,* Prince Genji puts a swarm of fireflies in a silk gauze bag and sneaks into the palace at night. He wishes to reveal his adoptive daughter, Tamakazura, to one of her suitors, who he has arranged to have visit her. When everything is ready, Genji pulls the cover off the silken bag and the glow of light reveals all.[73] It seems the idea of using bioluminescence as a flashlight was not so far fetched as it might seem at first.

In Gardens

As to whether there were fireflies in the gardens, in the Hahakigi chapter of *Genji Monogatari* fireflies are flitting about the garden of the Governor of Kii; and again, in the Maboroshi chapter, while Prince Genji is gazing out at the lotuses trying to get cool, the air is traced with the light of fireflies.[74] Scenes like these make clear that there were indeed fireflies in Heian-period gardens but, even if there was no literary evidence, we still could easily conclude that they were there. Almost all of the gardens of this period featured a pond, and if not a pond, at least they had a stream. Warblers and ducks found their way into the gardens as did fish. As far as fireflies went, the question is not "were they there" but "how could you keep them out?"

In Poetry

In poetry, the firefly can be called a *hotaru* or a *natsu-mushi*, the summer insect, and as the latter implies, the firefly is always an indicator of summer.

Ancient Japanese texts, such as the *Nihon Shoki, Chronicles of Japan*, portray the light of the firefly as being the embodiment of evil gods and the perception that those faint floating lights are the spirits of the dead persists to this day.[75] In poetry, however, *hotaru* is not an symbol of evil or the afterlife, but rather is used in conjunction with words such as *honoka*, faint or indistinct, and *moe*, burning (with light, and with desire).

In the Kashiwagi chapter of *Genji Monogatari*, there is a passage that compares an aged pine tree with a firefly in a roundabout way. Although the words *hotaru* or *natsu-mushi* are not used, a thousand year old pine, *senzai no matsu*, is presented as an image of eternity in comparison to "burning with a single remembrance," an allusion to a poem about a *natsu-mushi*.[76]

古今和歌集　562
　　紀友則

夕されば　螢よりけに　燃ゆれども　光見ねばや　人のつれなき
yū sareba　hotaru yorikeni　moyuredomo　hikari minebaya　hito no tsure naki

Kokin Wakashū 562

Ki no Tomonori

As evening falls
　　A burning grows inside me
　　　　a light to shame the fireflies
And yet, it lies unseen
　　by one as cold as you

後拾遺和歌集　216
　　源重之

音もせで　思ひにもゆる　螢こそ　なく虫よりも　あはれなりけれ
oto mo sede　omoi ni moyuru　hotaru koso　naku mushi yori mo　aware narikere

Goshūi Wakashū 216

Minamoto no Shigeyuki

So much more poignant
　　than those noisy crickets and cicadas
　　　　is the silent firefly
Glowing with remembrances
　　but saying nothing

Hototogisu ほととぎす Cuckoo

Hototogisu is the name of a bird as well as a plant, the toad lily (Tricyrtis hirta) that has striped patterns like the bird. These distinctive striped patterns gave the bird one of its lesser used nicknames, the *ayame-dori*, or "pattern-bird." Although *hototogisu* can refer to either the plant or the bird, Heian-period poems all refer to the bird, and there is no evidence that the plant was used in gardens at that time. The bird is the lesser cuckoo (Cuculus poliocephalus) a smaller variety of the common cuckoo, (*kakkō*, Cuculus canorus). There are at least ten different ways to write the word *hototogisu*, with the most common being either in *hiragana* (ほととぎす), or in one of the following three *kanji* combinations: 時鳥, 杜鵑, and 郭公. The last of these is also the way to write *kakkō*, the common cuckoo, adding to the confusion.

In the winter, the *hototogisu* lives in central-southern China and India, migrating to northern China, Korea, and Japan in the late spring and returning south again in the autumn. This appearance and disappearance from the natural environment formed the basis for some of the mythology associated with the bird. Their late arrival in the spring also is a cause of their well-known habit of brood parasitism by which they lay their eggs in the nests of other birds and allow those strangers to hatch and raise their young. This very distinctive characteristic, however, is not what Heian-period poets seem to have remembered.

It is the cry of the *hototogisu* that attracted the attention and fond thoughts of the Heian-period poets. A sweet, mournful repetitive trilling, it has a sound evocative of high-pitched human sobbing, thus the emotive quality. Being the first person to hear the cry in the spring was apparently a sign of good fortune.

In Gardens

In Heian-period literature the *hototogisu* is often associated with shrines. In both the *Murasaki Shikibu Nikki* and *Makura no Sōshi*, *hototogisu* are heard, or hoped to be heard, during visits to the Kamo Shrine.[77] Birds do fly, however, and there is no way to keep them out of gardens. In *Genji Monogatari*, for instance, Genji hears a *hototogisu* while peeking into the house of a woman near the Nakagawa River, and Kaoru hears one in the *tachibana* tree of his garden.[78] Both men are struck instantly upon hearing the cries to compose poems that incorporate *hototogisu* imagery.

In Poetry

In poems, *hototogisu* is used as a *makura-kotoba* linking to words such as *hotohoto*, meaning "nearly" as in the present-day *hotondo*, and *tobu*, meaning "to fly." From *tobu*, links are made to Tobata or Tobata no Ura, place names on the isle of Kyūshū. Because it is a five-syllable word, it makes a perfect "one-line" *makura-kotoba*. However, more than these direct connections, *hototogisu* is linked to other themes.

There are some things with which *hototogisu* are often linked. The most common are the *tachibana*, an orange tree (Citrus tachibana); *unohana*, also called *utsugi* (Deutzia crenata), a shrub with white flowers; *ayame*, the sweet rush (Acorus calamus); *uguisu*, Japanese bush warbler

(Cettia diphone); and, *satsuki*, the 5th month. Sei Shōnagon mentions *hototogisu* and *unohana* together often and says that the connection in poems between *hototogisu* and *tachibana* is so well-known, she has nothing more to add about it. An example of a poem with *hototogisu* and *ayame* together can be found in the previous section on *ayame*.

As mentioned before, the habit of *hototogisu* to migrate in and out of the area led to a particular mythology about the birds. They were believed to live in the mountains, begin their crying there in the 4th month, descend to the villages in the 5th month, and return to the mountains in the 6th month. This pattern transposed into a mythology of the bird traveling from the land of the dead, over the mountain of death (*shide no yama*, 死出の山), to visit the villagers planting their fields and encourage them with its bright song. This in turn led to another name for the *hototogisu*, Shide no Taosa, the Paddy Chief from the Land of Death.

There are many, many poems that feature the *hototogisu*, and although many do include the allegorical references mentioned here, overwhelmingly, it is the song of the bird, its sweet dulcet cry, and the pathos of waiting to hear that cry, that is the main theme of these poems.

古今和歌集 143
　　そせい
　　郭公のはじめてなきけるをききてよめる

郭公　はつこゑ聞けば　あぢきなく　主さだまらぬ　恋せらるはた

hototogisu　hatsukoe kikeba　ajikinaku　nushi sadamaranu　koiseraru hata

Kokin Wakashū 143
　　Sosei
　　Written upon hearing the first cry of the *hototogisu*

Oh *hototogisu*
　　I hear your first timid cries
　　　　　　and love pains stir　　wretched me
I've no one man in mind
　　and yet I love, and yet I love

金葉和歌集　104
　　修理大夫顕季
　　鳥羽殿の歌合に郭公をよめる

み山いでゝ　まだ里なれぬ　時鳥　たびのそらなる　音をやなくらん

miyama idede　mada satonarenu　hototogisu　tabi no sora naru　ne wo ya nakuran

Kin'yō Wakashū 104
　　Minister of Construction, Fujiwara no Akisue
　　Written about *hototogisu* at the poetry contest held by the
Emperor Toba

Fresh from the deep mountains
　　perhaps not yet used to village life
　　　　this *hototogisu*
Warbling in sweet tones
　　That are still high in the sky

HASU

hachisuba no
nigori ni shimanu
kokoro mote
nanika wa tsuyu wo
tama to azamuku
Kokin Wakashū 165

LOTUS

Noble lotus
even muddy waters can't stain
such a pure heart
Why then these deceits
conjuring jewels from dew-drops

Ike 池 Pond

The Element

The word for pond in Japanese is *ike* (池, pronounced *ee-keh*). Written with a different *kanji*, 生け, *ike* can also mean "giving life." It is thought the etymology of the word *ike*, meaning pond, is connected to the meaning of a "place of life." *Ike* can refer to anything from a small pool of water that you could throw a stone across to large bodies the size of lakes, from natural depressions in which water collects of its own accord to artificially dug arrangements made to hold water, much as the word pond does in English. The tradition of building artificial ponds for water storage is quite old. The *Nihon Shoki, Chronicles of Japan,* makes mention of the digging of ponds for agriculture as early as 33 BC during the reign of Emperor Sujin.[79]

Many of the natural ponds that the Heian-period courtiers would have known have long since disappeared. Ogura-ike, for instance, the huge pond to the south of the capital that acted as one of the four geomantic anchors for situating the city, was slowly encroached upon by the expanding city until, in a land reclamation program during the 1930s it was finally completely dried and filled in.

In the distant past, long before gardens were built in Japan, shrines of the native religion (now called Shintō) at times had ponds built on their precincts or were built next to existing ponds. These sacred ponds were called *kami-ike*, Pond of the Gods. A shrine structure was placed on an island in the pond to represent, in abstract form, an image of a distant land far across a broad sea from which the mythical ancestors of the Japanese people came.

In Gardens

In the history of garden building in Japan, the inclusion of artificial ponds in gardens shows up very early. The *Nihon Shoki, Chronicles of Japan,*

106

records the death in 626 of the great minister, Soga no Umako. He had, the passage goes on to say, a residence on the banks of the Asuka River that had a pond with an island in it. This garden was so well known, he became known as Shima no Ōomi, The Minister of the Island. This is one of the first recorded garden ponds in Japan.[80]

There is ample evidence of ponds in gardens in the Heian period. Archeological digs of Heian-period residences often show the remains of ponds. A common technique at that time was to line the bottom surface of the pond with fist-sized stones to keep the mud from mixing into the water. These layers of stones are relatively easy to ascertain in a dig, allowing not only the existence of the pond but also their size and shape to be determined with some accuracy.

The *Sakuteiki* goes to some length to describe how a pond should be created, including how to use a Water Level device to lay out the pond, what height to set the surface level of the pond in reference to the Fishing Pavilion, how to set stones in a pond so they won't tip over, what direction to cause the water to flow through the pond, the meandering shapes that the edges of the pond should take, and how to make the pond bank look like a rough ocean coast. Ponds were thought best to be shallow (so the fish wouldn't grow too big) and fortuitous when filled with water fowl (which would bring blessings to the master of the house). Finally, there is an interesting point that shows the degree of importance the pond held, in geomantic terms, in the minds of the Heian-period courtiers. The *Sakuteiki* points out that water will take the shape of any vessel it is put into and that, according to that shape, the pond will bring good or bad fortune.[81] The *Sakuteiki*, therefore, suggests that there were both geomantic and aesthetic concerns when designing a garden pond.

In *Genji Monogatari*, ponds appear in gardens numerous times. We see garden ponds with lotuses covering their surface, those slicked with ice, ones in which the ice has just melted and willows overhang the banks, ponds busy with flocks of waterfowl chattering away, another choked with weeds in an ancient overgrown garden, broad ponds with moonlight cast over them, music being played on ponds by musicians in Chinese-style boats with prows carved like dragons and mythical birds, people out in garden pavilions enjoying the cool air above the water, even ponds that have cormorant fishermen on them hunting for fish.[82]

When Sei Shōnagon lists ponds, she doesn't list garden ponds but rather those out in the countryside. She does, however, mention garden ponds in other places, almost always in connection with lotuses. In her list of "Things that Recall the Past but no Longer Have a Purpose," she includes an overgrown garden choked with weeds. Interestingly, she gives a similar example — an overgrown garden with a pond choked with weeds — as being appropriate for a woman who lives alone, since it conveys the right tone of piteousness.[83]

In Poetry

In poetry, the expression *ikemizu no*, of the waters of the pond, is a *makura-kotoba* that leads to various words: *ii* (an ancient word for a pipe that controlled the flow of water in or out of a pond), *soko* (bottom), *shita* (underneath), and *fukaki* (deep). It is also an *engo* that is linked to *mizukakuru*, to be hidden under water.

More than these specific meanings, however, ponds are associated with images of emotional depth or emotional reflection, for obvious reasons. The pond is also just a very compelling setting to which people are drawn — the place of life. As such, ponds show up in poems simply as romantic, beautiful places.

拾遺和歌集　1221
　　明日香の采女　　返し

池水の　そこにあらでは　ねぬなはの　来る人もなし　待つ人もなし

ikemizu no　soko ni arade wa　nenunawa no　kuru hito mo nashi　matsu hito mo nashi

　　Shūi Wakashū 1221
　　　　A Response by Asuka no Uneme

The pond bottom
　　may be thick with twisted roots
　　　　but I have no entanglements
I wait for no one else
　　and no one else comes

金葉和歌集　85
　　大納言經信
　　二條關白の家に池邊藤花といへる事をよめる

池にひづ　松の延枝に　むらさきの　波をりかくる　藤さきにけり

ike ni hizu　matsu no haie ni　murasaki no　nami ori kakuru　fuji sakinikeri

　　Kin'yō Wakashū 85
　　　　Vice Council of State Tsunenobu
　　　　Written about the wisteria near the pond at the house of
Nijō Kampaku, Chief Advisor to the Emperor

Reaching low to touch the pond
　　the outstretched arms of the pine tree
　　　　cast out shimmering violet
Folded, rippling waves
　　laden with tresses of wisteria

Iwa 岩 巖 磐 Stone

The Element

Japan is a mountainous island country sliced by many deep valleys with swift rivers and a long, jagged ocean coastline. Needless to say, there are stones of all sizes exposed everywhere from mountain top crags to river boulders to rocky shores along the ocean. Accordingly, the imagery and vocabulary of stones shows up in many places: in mythology, place names, personal names, names of gods, poetic symbols, and, of course, in gardens.

In ancient Shintō ritual prayers we find the words for stones related to, as one might expect, images of both perpetuity and strength. Before religious architecture developed in Japan there was a culture of using elements of the natural world as sites for religious gatherings. This practice remains to some extent to this day and the elements include ancient large trees, waterfalls, ponds, and stones. The stones may be large or small, single or grouped, but are referred to most commonly by the term *iwakura* (磐座). The *iwakura* are seen as a medium between the world of the gods (or the realm of the afterlife) and the world of temporal existence.

In Gardens

We know that stones were used in gardens in the Heian period, and how they were used, in some ways better than any other aspect of the gardens. The reason is simple — stones don't rot away. Archeological digs of Heian-period gardens often reveal garden stones in the same position as they were nearly a thousand years ago. We also know a great deal from literature, most importantly from the *Sakuteiki*.

The first line of the *Sakuteki* reads *ishi wo taten koto*, the "art of setting stones," in other words, the "art of making gardens." There was no expression for gardening other than that of "setting stones" because the placement and arrangement of stones was the primary act of gardening. Stones were placed in gardens for their beauty — the aesthetic component

— but they also held other meanings. A section of the *Sakuteiki* called "Secret Teachings on Setting Stones" has this to say.

> When setting stones, first bring a number of different stones, both large and small, to the garden site and temporarily set them out on the ground. Set those that will be standing stones with their "heads" upright, and those that will be reclining stones with their best side facing out. Compare the various qualities of the stones and, keeping the overall garden plan in mind, pull the stones into place one by one.[84]

Some stones were described in the *Sakuteiki* as being the embodiment of Buddhist deities, such as the Buddhist Trinty stone or the waterfall stones which were perceived as the image of Fudō Myōō.

> According to the Rituals of Fudō: "Those who see my form, aspire to enlightenment. Those who hear my name, reject evil and master virtue," and so forth. Thus the name Fudō, The Unmovable. In order to behold my form it is not necessary to know the form of Shōkoku Dōji. Always be aware of waterfalls, for although Fudō Myōō takes many forms, the most fundamental of all these are waterfalls.[85]

Others held meaning, according to the *Sakuteiki*, within the context of Chinese geomancy, *in'yō gogyō setsu* (陰陽五行説), and were selected for their color or size and placed in specific cardinal directions according to geomantic teachings.

> Do not set a white stone that is bigger than those around it in the easterly direction or harm will come to the master of the house. Likewise, in all other directions, be careful not to set stones that are of "controlling" colors nor ones that are larger than the other stones there.[86]

Still other stones mentioned in the *Sakuteiki* were related to local

Japanese taboos, *mono imi*, that dictated what should or should not be done.

> Regarding the placement of stones there are many taboos. If so much as one of these taboos is violated, the master of the household will fall ill and eventually die, and his land will fall into desolation and become the abode of devils. [One such taboo is...] using a stone that once stood upright in a reclining manner or using a reclining stone as a standing stone. If this is done, that stone will definitely become a Phantom Stone and be cursed.[87]

In *Genji Monogatari,* we find many references to stones in gardens — beautiful stones in streams, massive boulders in an island cove.[88] Stones are, at times, described as beautiful or impressive, but they do not carry any of the particular geomantic or Buddhist meanings mentioned above. Likewise, stones do not feature as prominently in *Genji Monogatari* as do garden plants. From a comparison of the *Sakuteiki* and books like *Genji Monogatari*, we are left with two contrasting images of stones in gardens — one in which their use is considered with deadly seriousness (literally) and the other in which they are seen as simply part of the fabric of the overall garden.

In Poetry

The use of the word *iwa*, or variations thereof, in poetry is common and complex. There are many place names that include the word *iwa* in them and so we find that at least half of the *makura-kotoba* associated with *iwa* are in fact related to a place name containing *iwa* and not to a stone. Some of the *makura-kotoba* do refer to actual stones such as *iwa bashiru*, which literally means "running over rocks," an image of water splashing in a torrent over rocks, and links to words such as *tarumi*, waterfall. Another is *iwane*, rock roots, or *iwane no matsu*, pines by well-rooted stones, both of which are images of strength, vigor, tenaciousness, and long life.

万葉集　1142

命をし　幸く良けむと　石走る　垂水の水を　むすびて飲みつ
inochi wo shi　sakiku yokemu to　iwabashiru　tarumi no mizu wo　musubite nomitsu

Man'yōshū 1142

Wild water　　rushing over rocks
　　falling fast in quick leaps
　　　　I scoop a handful and drink
　Binding a prayer
　　for a fortunate life

拾遺和歌集　273
　　兼盛
　　天暦のみかど四十になりおはしましける時山階寺に金泥壽命經四十
八卷をかき供養し奉りて御卷數鶴にくはせてすはまにたてたりけり。其すは
まのしき物にあまたの歌あしてにかける中に

山階の　山の岩根に　松植へて　ときはかきはに　祈りつる哉
yama shina no　yama no iwa ne ni　matsu uete　tokiwa kakiwa ni　inoritsuru kana

Shūi Wakashū 273
　　Kanemori
　　On the occasion of Emperor Murakami turning 40 years of age, 48
volumes of the Jumyō Sutra were copied out in gold letters and consecrated
to Yamashina Temple. The catalogue of this work was placed in the bill of [an
artificial] crane, which was set on a tray seascape (*suhama*). Poems brushed in a
free-flowing hand over a marsh landscape (*ashide*) were also placed on the tray,
including this one.

At the base of a sturdy boulder
　　on Yamashina mountain
　　　　I planted a pine tree
　And prayed that our lord
　　may live as long and be as strong

Kaki 垣 Fence

A *kaki* is a fence or a hedge, not to be confused with the homonym, *kaki*, that means persimmon (or the other *kaki* that means oyster). There are many variations of this word that show up in the literature of the Heian period or before. At times, the word *kaki* (垣) was used by itself and in other situations it appears in combination with other words, such as *kakine* (垣根), in which case *kaki* is paired with *ne*, the word for "root." *Kakine* is the most common expression used nowadays to mean fence although it was only one of many in the Heian period and not the most common at that. The most commonly occurring expression for fence were the words *magaki* (籬) and *masegaki* (籬垣). These both refer to simple rustic fences that were loosely built of grass, reeds, bamboo, or the like. Another such expression, *aragaki* (荒垣), simply means "rough fence," while others specify the building material such as *shibagaki* (柴垣), a fence made of brushwood or twigs, and *ashigaki* (葦垣), a fence made of reeds. The often mentioned *suigai* or *suigaki* (透垣), literally "see-through fence," refers to the open weave that offers only partial visual obstruction. There are also a number of fences mentioned that were used to mark off sacred precincts at shrines with names such as *igaki* or *imigaki* (斎垣・齋垣, sacred fence), *mizugaki* (瑞垣, felicitous fence), and *tamagaki* (玉垣, jewel fence).

The word *kaki* is also used in Heian-period literature in combination with the names of plants. This happens in such a way that it is not always clear whether what is being described is a fence with plants growing along it, a lattice-like structure with plants grown on it, or a living fence, in other words a hedge. *Unohana*, Deutzia crenata, for instance, is mentioned by Sei Shōnagon as flowering in the rustic *kakine* of the houses in the Murasaki district.[89] By this, she most likely meant a hedge made entirely of the shrub albeit loosely pruned if pruned at all. The same thing can be said for the reference in the Otome chapter of *Genji Monogatari* to *unohana no kakine*, and in the Kochō chapter to *yamabuki no magaki*, a fence made of *yamabuki*, Kerria japonica.[90] *Yamabuki*, like *unohana*, could make a hedge of its own accord, which would have been, as with *unohana*, a loose hedge rather than a tightly clipped one.

Also in the Otome chapter of *Genji Monogatari*, we find mention of *kiku no magaki*, chrysanthemum fence, but chrysanthemum are too small to make a fence by themselves, so this must refer to a fence with chrysanthemum growing up through it or a fence that has chrysanthemum planted along the base and named after the plant that runs along it.[91] Sei Shōnagon mentions a sacred fence, *igaki*, around Hirano Shrine that was covered with ivy (*tsuta*), deep in its fall color, so this brings to mind a well-built, rigid structure with vines weaving in and out of it.[92]

In Gardens

There are many instances of people noticing fences in gardens in Heian-period literature or standing behind them to peek out at someone they are infatuated with. Again, it is often difficult to ascertain exactly what the design of these fences was. But there are, as mentioned above, basically four possibilities: fences constructed out of some material such as bamboo, reeds, or branches; a constructed fence or lattice-structure with living plants or vines growing interwoven into the fence; a constructed fence with vegetation planted all along its base; and a living fence or hedge made with shrubs planted in rows. Most likely, all of these possibilities existed and the language simply does not make a point of specifying which is which.

Genji Monogatari provides many example of fences used in gardens. In the Hahakigi chapter, for instance, when Genji drops in suddenly at the house of the Governor of Kii, he finds in the garden a brushwood fence, *shibagaki*, that evokes the atmosphere of a country farmhouse. In the Hanachirusato chapter there is a mention of *ueshi no kakine*, a "planted fence," which very likely refers to a hedge. In the Suma chapter, in which

115

Genji is in self-exile in Suma, a two-days' journey from the capital, he lives in a house that is described as being of a Chinese-style design that had a fence made of woven bamboo, *take ameru kaki*. The Nowaki chapter begins with a description of the garden Genji had built for Akikonomu in which flowers of many colors and types are seen weaving through fences of wood, some peeled of their bark, some not. In the Makibashira chapter, a fence of Chinese bamboo, *kuretake no magaki*, is described covered in the blossoms of kerria and wisteria. [93]

In Poetry

The fence in Heian-period poetry is used in one of several ways. First, there is the fence simply as an object, often one upon which other things that are more central to the poem — flowers, snow, etc. — play out their part. Presented alone or in combination with other things, fences are often used to create a sense of earthy rusticity or pastoral calm. Flowers blooming in a rough fence/hedge, even if it is in the urban garden of an aristocratic family, evoke the image of a country village settled gently into the natural world and the simple homes of peasant folk living close to the land.

A second way fences are presented is as a symbol of enclosure and protection. This is particularly true of the fences that surround religious spaces, as mentioned above, although the mountains of Japan themselves have also been depicted as a Green Fence, *aogaki*, within which the lands and people of Japan are protected and peacefully settled. Examples of this can be found in the *Man'yōshū* and even as far back as the *Kojiki*. [94]

The third depiction is the fence as a symbol of division or separation, in particular as an allegory for some aspect of life that bars two lovers from meeting. In the Sakaki chapter of *Genji Monogatari*, Genji follows one of his past lovers, the Lady Rokujō, to a country shrine. She was the widow of a Crown Prince and as such, Genji's past affections and approaches toward her were socially unacceptable. During their meeting at the shrine, their conversation is peppered with references to an *igaki*, sacred fence, which they use as a symbol of the line of propriety that existed between them that had been breached in the past.[95]

The idea of the fence as a thing existing between lovers is intertwined with the Heian-period concept of *kaimami*, literally, "peeping through the gap of a fence." *Kaimami* is a kind of voyeurism that existed because of certain constraints characteristic of Heian-period society. Women of the aristocratic class were expected to be demure and withdrawing to a fault. They were not supposed to allow themselves to be seen by anyone outside a small inner circle of family relations and attendants, if those. As such, they spent much of the daytime withdrawn behind curtains and screens. Aristocratic men, as one might expect, were desperate to catch a glimpse of one of these hidden angels whom they could only imagine. It is here that the lowly garden fence steps in to provide the solution. The part of the garden closest to the rooms of the residences was called the "near garden," *senzai* (前栽), *omae* (御前), or the combined *omae no senzai*. In the near garden were found flowers and grasses, some trees and occasional fences that either divided off sections of the garden into private areas or simply improved the view, providing an air of rusticity. The aristocratic residences were all one-story wooden buildings and the walls that faced the gardens were made of large lattice panels that could be fully opened, allowing for an unobstructed view of the garden — or, in reverse, a view from the garden into the inner rooms. The voyeuristic practice of *kaimami* shows up time and time again in Heian-period literature in scenes where ardently affectionate would-be paramours — or creepy, peeping Toms depending on one's take on things — sidled up to the fences to take their chances at getting a look at a princess or lady-in-waiting. *Ise Monogatari* begins with such a scene and, in *Genji Monogatari*, Genji finds, and eventually absconds with, his child-lover Murasaki in this way.[96]

古今和歌集　506

人知れぬ　思ひやなぞと　葦垣の　まぢかけれども　逢ふよしのなき
hitoshirenu　omoi ya nazo to　ashigaki no　majikakeredomo　au yoshi no naki

Kokin Wakashū 506

We are so close
　　　separated by no more than a reed fence
　　　　　and yet, still cannot meet
What good this thing —
　　　a love unspoken

万葉集 713
　　丹波大女娘子

垣穂なす　人言聞きて　我が背子が　心たゆたひ　逢はぬこのころ
kakiho nasu　hitogoto kikite　waga seko ga　kokoro tayutai　awanu kono koro

Man'yōshū 713
　　Taniha no Ōme no Otome

His heart wavers —
　　　I don't see him these days
　　　　　this man I love
Shuttered by tall fences
　　　of lies and innuendo

Kakitsubata 杜若 *Japanese Iris*

Kakitsubata, the Japanese water iris, is an aquatic plant that grows a little over 60 centimeters (2 feet) in height. The botanical name is Iris laevigata. It is often found growing over broad areas of low water in ponds or marshes, or along riverbanks. In May/June it sets a brilliant blue-purple flower and the sight of thousands of these plants in full bloom together is truly breathtaking.

The name *kakitsubata* derives from *kaki-tsuke-bana*, a "flower to rub and dye with," as in the modern expression *kosuri-tsukeru*. This name stems from the fact that the flower could be rubbed against cloth to transfer the color as a purple dye, one of the first dyestuffs recorded in Japan.

In Gardens

The word *kakitsubata* shows up in the *Sakuteiki*, which suggests using it, along with *ayame*, in the creation of the Wetland Style of gardening.[97] This passage makes it very clear that *kakitsubata* were used in gardens in the Heian period but, in fact, there is little other evidence that links the plant with gardens. It isn't mentioned in *Genji Monogatari* and Sei Shōnagon simply says that that, among purple flowers, she likes the *kakitsubata* only a little.

In Poetry

Kakitsubata is used as a *makura-kotoba* to link to *saku*, the verb "to flower," the connection to which is obvious, and to *nitsurau*, to have a beautiful "red" face, which is less so. Although the courtly culture of the Heian period typically favored pale skin as being lovely, these older poems seem to express an appreciation for a ruddier beauty. In hearing *nitsurau* one imagines a healthy, vigorous outdoor beauty, cheeks flushed and full of life.

Kakitsubata is also famously linked to a particular place known as Yatsuhashi, or the Eight Bridges. The *Ise Monogatari*, *Tales of Ise*, a mid-10[98]-century collection of lyrical episodes, records a scene in Mikawa (present-day Aichi Prefecture) where a river splits into smaller streams like a "spider's web" and eight bridges had been built to cross the streams.[98] *Kakitsubata* grew in the marshes near the streams making for a beautiful sight. The text then goes on to introduce what is now the most famous poem related to *kakitsubata*. Unfortunately it doesn't translate well because the poem does not actually mention *kakitsubata*, the plant, instead the first syllable of each of the five lines reads *ka ki tsu ba ta*. In any case, the poetic connection between *kakitsubata* and marshland crossed by bridges is ancient. In public parks in Japan today one often finds an area of low water crossed by a stereotypic zig-zag eight-planked bridge, but the irises planted around them are usually, Iris ensata not Iris laevigata — the ancient poetic connection having been forgotten by park administrators.

万葉集　2521

かきつばた　につらふ君を　ゆくりなく　思ひ出でつつ　嘆きつるかも
kakitsubata　nitsurau kimi wo　yukurinaku　omoiidetsutsu,　nagekitsuru kamo

Man'yōshū 2521

Ah sweet iris
　　your face flushed pink
Unexpectedly
　　I remember you
　　　　and sigh

☙　　❧

万葉集　3052

かきつばた　佐紀沢に生ふる　菅の根の　絶ゆとや君が　見えぬこのころ
kakitsubata　saku sawa ni ouru　suga no ne no　tayu to ya kimi ga　mienu kono koro

Man'yōshū 3052

Is it the end
　　for all the sedge grass roots
　　　　that grow amid the iris in the marsh
Is it the end
　　I don't see you these days

Kasumi Kiri 霞 霧 Mist Fog

The Element

The words *kasumi* and *kiri* are often interchangeably translated as mist, haze, or fog. *Kasumi* is usually used to express a lighter entity (made of smaller droplets of water) at times when it's warm, so the word haze would be really best here, while *kiri* is used to mean something that is somewhat heavier, hanging lower to the ground, often on chilly mornings or evenings, so fog might be more appropriate. Mist could work for either word. After rains, the peaked mountains of Japan will poke their summits out from trailing swathes of mist, looking very much like a classical ink landscape painting. This is especially true in spring and autumn, which, as we shall see, underlies the poetic metaphors related to these elements.

In Gardens

Mist of course forms where it pleases, so it can be assumed it appeared in Heian-period gardens as well. In *Genji Monogatari* we find many scenes where gardens are "robed in mists" such as that at the end of the Suetsumu-hana chapter where Genji plays with young Murasaki at his Nijō palace while the trees in the spring garden are covered in mist, the plums blooming beautifully. In this case the word *kasumi* was used.[99] Or, in the Young Murasaki chapter where Prince Genji finds himself wrapped in a thick morning fog — in this case the word *kiri* was used — and is moved to use fog as the theme for a poem sung out over a locked gate to announce his arrival to a woman he wishes to visit. She answers with a poem in the negative but manages somehow to work the theme of fog into her rebuff.[100] The fact that most Heian-period gardens of any size featured a central pond would have increased the likelihood that mist could form there in the morning and evening. Sei Shōnagon, in *Makura no Sōshi*, mentions the women of court walking about in the garden at dawn on a brisk autumn morning when the moon still hung in the sky. The garden, she notes, was beautifully draped with mists.[101]

In Poetry

In older poetic anthologies, such as the *Man'yōshū*, kasumi and kiri are used in poems of both autumn and spring, but by the Heian period, a poetic convention of *aki no kiri, haru no kasumi*, autumn fog and spring haze, had developed. This is borne out in the aforementioned examples, where in the *Genji Monogatari* chapters, which were about spring, the word used was *kasumi*, and in *Makura no Sōshi*, which was set in autumn, the word was *kiri*.

Because of the quality of mists which makes it difficult to see, as one might well imagine, *kasumi* and *kiri* became poetically linked with the idea of hidden things, things veiled from sight, or things not clearly ascertainable. The word *kasumi* is related to the word *kasuka*, meaning faint, dim, or indistinct, and the image of *kasumi* in poetry is often used to create a sense of things unknown. *Kiri* is at times described as hiding things from each other in a somewhat willful way, as with separating two lovers from each other almost intentionally. There is a poetic expression, *kiri no magaki*, the fence woven of mists, that is used in this fashion. There are also examples of *kasumi no magaki*, though less common.

古今和歌集　479
　　　紀貫之
　　人の花つみしける所にまかりて、そこなりける人のもとに、のちに
よみてつかはしける

山ざくら　霞の間より　ほのかにも　見てし人こそ　恋しかりけれ
yamazakura　kasumi no ma yori　honoka ni mo　miteshi hito koso　koishikarikere

　　Kokin Wakashū 479
　　　Ki no Tsurayuki
　　　By chance, having seen a woman pluck a flower, I sent
this poem to her house

　　Just a passing glimpse of her
　　　　no more than a hint
　　Mountain cherry flowers
　　　　seen through parting veils of mist
　　　　　　and here I am　　fast in love

古今和歌集　935

雁のくる　峯の朝霧　はれずのみ　思ひ尽きせぬ　世の中の憂さ
kari no kuru　mine no asagiri　harezu nomi　omoi tsukisenu　yo no naka no usa

　　Kokin Wakashū 935

　　Geese fly slowly my way
　　　　over peaks shrouded by morning mist
　　　　　　with no hope of clearing　　clinging
　　These endless desperate thoughts
　　　　the sadness of the world

Katsumi　かつみ　Iris, Wild Rice

The Element

There are several diverging theories as to which plant the word *katsumi*, or *hana-katsumi* as it is also called, refers to. The two most likely possibilities are the Japanese water iris, now called *no-hana-shōbu*, and Manchurian wild rice, now called *makomo*. The water iris (Iris ensata var. spontanea) grows along the banks of ponds and streams as well as in wetland areas. Its three-petalled flower is a brilliant red-purple with a dash of yellow at the base. They are not nearly as showy as the modern horticultural varieties that are seen commonly today in large Japanese parks and stroll gardens, but in the Heian period, before so many show-flowers had been bred, the *no-hana-shōbu* must have seemed very showy indeed.

The other possibility, Manchurian wild rice (Zizania latifolia), is not a showy plant in the least. It too grows in wetland areas and along water's edges but it does not have a prominent flower at all. The stalks of the *makomo* can become infected with a smut fungus, Ustilago esculenta. The infected culms swell and are harvested as a vegetable called *makomo-take*. The black spores of this fungus are used as a pigment in lacquerware.

In Gardens

There is little evidence in the usual sources to show that *katsumi* was actually used in gardens during the Heian period, except for the most trusted source, the *Sakuteiki*, which suggests it as one of the plants to be used when creating a wetlands scene within a garden. This is the only direct evidence that *katsumi* was planted in gardens.

In Poetry

The word *katsumi* can be linked poetically to words that it sounds like, such as *katsute*, formerly. More than this kind of word play, however, *katsumi*, whether it be the iris or the wild rice, is symbolically linked to wetlands.

万葉集　675
　　中臣郎女、大伴宿禰家持に送る歌五首

をみなへし　佐紀沢に生ふる　花かつみ　かつても知らぬ　恋もするかも
ominaeshi　saku sawa ni ouru　hanakatsumi　katsute mo shiranu　koi mo suru kamo

    Man'yōshū 675
        One of Five Poems that Lady Nakatomi no Iratsume sent
to Ōtomo no Yakamochi

    In the marsh where flower
        pale maidenflowers
            I plucked a radiant iris
    Not once before
        have I felt a love this deep

千載集　436
　　賀茂重保

をく霜を　はらひかねてや　しほれふす　かつみがしたに　鴛のなくらん
oku shimo wo　haraikanete ya　shiorefusu　katsumi ga shita ni　oshi no nakuran

    Senzaishū 436
    Kamo no Shigeyasu

    A hard frost settles
        too much to be brushed off
    From beneath the wild rice stalks
        now withered and bent
            is that the cry of the Mandarin ducks

Kawa 川 河 River

Kawa means river, and rivers need no introduction other than to explain how the natural environment of Japan has influenced its rivers. Japan is a mountainous country with steep hills and narrow valleys. This, combined with generous annual precipitation, allows for a lot of quick surface runoff. Because Japan is a relatively small country, there is not a great distance between the head of a river in the mountains and the point where it empties into the sea. These factors mean that there are many rivers in Japan — large and small — that are typically shallow and quick. When it rains, the rivers fill quickly, at times overflow, and then drain back down to their typical shallow flow in a short time. The larger rivers were navigable by boat at their lower reaches primarily because Japanese river boats had a relatively shallow draw.

Traveling through the countryside of Japan, as many poets did, meant encountering rivers: crossing them at fords or bridges, traveling along them (since many roads and footpaths paralleled rivers), or riding up and down them in river boats. As such the imagery of rivers proved to be useful stock for the poet.

In Gardens

We know from many sources that streams have been a part of Japanese gardens from the earliest times. River is too grandiose a word to describe what actually existed in the gardens because the scale of Japanese gardens did not allow for anything so large as a river but, conceptually, as we shall see, the intention of the garden designer was at times to evoke the image of a stream and at others to evoke a broad river.

Well before the Heian period, streams were used in gardens. Records for the 1st day of the 3rd month for 485, 486, and 487, during the reign of

Emperor Kenzō, relate that on at least these three occasions the Emperor gathered people at a garden and held a Festival by the Winding Stream, *kyokusui no en*.[102] This Festival was a poetic competition of sorts in which poets sit along a convoluted, meandering stream, undoubtedly one built for the purpose, and attempt to compose a poem on a given theme on-the-spot before wine cups floated down the stream, or a toy boat laden with wine cups, reach them. Archeological digs of gardens of the Nara period reveal that some featured a long winding stream, lined with large pebbles and some boulders, as a central part of the garden.

We also know about streams in Heian-period gardens from several sources including literature, such as the *Sakuteiki, Genji Monogatari,* and *Makura no Sōshi,* and archeological digs. The *Sakuteiki* mentions several types of streams. One of the most common expressions used is *yarimizu*. The word *yari* means to send or dispatch and *mizu* means water, so *yarimizu* refers to any artificially-built stream or channel. The descriptions in the *Sakuteiki*, however, are not of artificial channel-like streams. Instead, they describe very naturalistic designs, with stones set in certain ways to modulate the flow of water that had names such as Water-Splitting Stones, Crosswise Stones, and Spillway Stones.[103]

The direction of the flow was important according to the geomantic design systems of the day. In general, water was allowed to enter a property in the north or northeast, from where it would flow between various buildings on the eastern side of the property passing between the central hall and an eastern auxiliary hall. When it reached the south-eastern portion of the property it would turn toward the west and enter a large pond that was situated centrally on the southern part of the property, pass through the pond, and eventually flow out in the south-western section of the property.

The *Sakuteiki* also mentions certain styles of gardening based on stream or river motifs: the Broad River style (*ōkawa no yō,* 大河の様),

the Mountain Torrent style (*yamagawa no yō*, 山河の様), and the Valley Stream style (*tanigawa no yō*, 谷川の様). The key to the Broad River style was to make it meander like the slow movements of a river where it broadens in its lower reaches; the Mountain Torrent style required many stones in the stream to make the water moving through roil and burble like a quick-moving mountain stream; and the Valley Stream is one where the stream would come splashing out from in between two hillocks built up in the garden.[104]

Genji Monogatari and *Murasaki Shikibu Nikki* both mention streams in the gardens of the characters in the story, which are usually referred to as *yarimizu* rather than *kawa*. Interestingly enough, at least twice in each story, one of the characters, a person of very high rank, is described as supervising or ordering the clearing of debris from a garden stream — Prince Genji in the Matsukaze chapter and Yūgiri, Genji's son, in the Fuji no Uraba chapter. No other form of garden maintenance, such as pruning trees and shrubs, is described in either book. For some reason, the streams were close enough to the lives of the residents — both physically and emotionally — that they would engage in its care directly.[105]

In Poetry

Rivers came to be associated with the landscapes and histories of the localities they flowed through. Poets began to use the names of rivers as *uta-makura*, place names that evoke the larger story of their locale. Three of the most famous are the Uji River (宇治川), the Tatsuta River (龍田川), and the Ōi River(大堰川). The Uji River, which is south of where the capital Heian lay, is fed by waters from Lake Biwa, merges with the Kizu and Katsura Rivers and then flows on to the sea at Ōsaka. As part of the river boat transportation system it was well known to the people of the capital. Poets remember the bridge at Uji (*ujigawa no hashi*: see the previous section on *hashi*), the mist that hangs over the river (*kawagiri*), waves on the water (*uji no kawanami*), and so on. That fact that two words meaning gloomy and grief, *ui* and *urei*, have the same distinctive "*u*" sound as Uji, forms a poetic link between Uji and images of pathos. The Tatsuta River is linked most often to autumn colors, especially the brightly colored leaves it carries away in its current. The Ōi River lies just west of where the Heian capital was situated. It flows out of the mountains to the northwest, fast and wild, then slows down on the plain as it broadens. There, its name changes to the Katsura River. Two favorite themes that poets incorporated into poems along with the Ōi River are the river boats, or rafts, that carried timber from the mountains down the fast river to the capital below, and the autumn colors of the mountains that frame the steep valleys that the river flows through. There are also some rivers in poems that are not real but whose names have specific poetic meanings such as Omoigawa (思川, River of Remembrance), Amanogawa (天の川, the River of Heaven),[106] and the ever popular Namidagawa (涙川, River of Tears).

Some poems about rivers seem to simply want to capture the sheer beauty of nature — the gentle flow of water, plum blossoms or red maple leaves drifting in the stream. However, the flow of water in rivers was used in other poems for symbolic reasons such as marking the passage of time. Poems of praise, for instance, wishing long life upon an important personage, may include the image of a river to mean, "may you live as long as this river runs." In love poems, the flow would symbolize not time but the inner feelings of the poet: choppy waves on a river for emotional turmoil, quick waters for the onrush of sudden love, hidden waters for secret admiration, or powerful currents for irresistible love.

古今和歌集 607
　　紀友則

言にいでて　言はぬばかりぞ　水無瀬川　したにかよひて　恋しきものを
koto ni idete iwanu bakari zo minasegawa shita ni kayoite koishiki mono wo

　　Kokin Wakashū 607
　　　Ki noTomonori

　　This thing I would say
　　　　remains unspoken
　　　　　　to the one I love
　　Hidden within　　yet constantly flowing
　　　　like an underground river

山家集　　873
　　西行
　　人命不停速於山水の文の心を

山川の　みなぎる水の　音聞けば　迫むる命ぞ　おもひ知らるゝ
yamagawa no   minagiru mizu no   oto kikeba   semuru inochi zo   omoi shiraruru

　　Sankashū 873
　　　Saigyō
　　Composed on the theme of how human existence flows, never-
　　stopping, faster than a mountain stream

　　Listening to waters
　　　　cascade in swollen torrents
　　　　　　down the mountain
　　It all comes clear —
　　　　how quickly life passes

Kawazu かはづ Frog

The Element

Kawazu is an old form of the word *kaeru* meaning frog. There is some debate, however, as to which kind of frog *kawazu* refers to. One explanation is that *kawazu* referred to frogs in general and another holds that it referred only to a small river frog now called *kajika*, Buergeria buergeri. The *kanji* used to write *kajika* means "river deer." Some poetic references link the call of the *kawazu* with the classical image of a stag crying for its mate. This would support the idea that *kawazu* and *kajika* are one and the same, and that may be true, but the actual call of the *kajka*, unlike the piercing mournful bellow of the deer, is a high stuttering whistling that sounds somewhat more like a cricket's chirp than a frog's croak.

Frogs in Japan are found everywhere — in bogs, streams, grassy meadows, even in trees. The *kajika*, however, is found primarily in rushing clear streams. The scenes described in many poems about *kawazu* are of this sort of quick-flowing stream, giving another clue that the frog described may have been a *kajika* in particular rather than any other type of frog.

In Gardens

The water systems of Heian-period gardens were linked to one another. In general, water was brought into the capital from rivers and streams in the north or northeast, and flowed down through the city to the south and southwest in a series of large and small roadside channels. Individual properties would allow this water to flow in through a small hole in the surrounding earthen wall in the north or northeast, bring it through the property in an arc — north/northeast to east to south to southwest — and then allow it to exit the property into a roadside channel and, eventually,

132

on to the next residence.[107] Naturally, any water animals, be they fish or frogs, could flow with the water from the wild, through various properties, and perhaps back to the wild again. Sei Shōnagon mentions that a frog even made its way up into the palace — and jumped straight into a brazier, burning up in smoke. Even that, it turns out, was inspiration for thinking up a poem on the spot!

In Poetry

As mentioned in the introduction to this book, in the preface to the *Kokinshū*, Ki no Tsurayuki wrote, "He who hears ... a frog crying from its watery home, who could live among such living things and not want to write a poem?"[108] It would seem that to the Heian courtiers, the cry of the frog was synonymous with poetic sentiment.

In poetry, *kawazu* was most often linked to the season of spring. It was also inevitably linked to the image of streams or springs, and places that were well-known to have clear streams or abundant springs. In poetry of the Heian period, *kawazu* is, at times, associated with a shrub called the *yamabuki*, Kerria japonica. The *yamabuki* is often found along waterways and is described that way in poetry (see the section on *yamabuki* below), making the connection between *yamabuki* and *kawazu* a natural one.

万葉集　2164

瀬を速み　落ち激ちたる　白波に　かはづ鳴くなり　朝夕ごとに
se wo hayami　ochitagichitaru　shiranami ni　kawazu nakunari　asayū goto ni

Man'yōshū 2164

The torrent　　runs swift in the shallows
　　　　so tumbles down　　seething
　　　　　　in quick white waves
The song of the *kawazu* comes sweetly
　　　crying morning　　crying night

古今和歌集　125
　　よみ人しらず

かはづ鳴く　井手の山吹　散りにけり　花のさかりに　あはましものを
kawazu naku　ide no yamabuki　chirinikeri　hana no sakari ni　awamashi mono wo

Kokin Wakashū 125
　　Anonymous

The sweet river frog cries
　　　among the scattered blossoms
　　　　　of *yamabuki* near Ide village
Too late　　these flowers are best seen
　　　in cascades of full bloom

Kiku 菊 Chrysanthemum

The Element

Nowadays, the word *kiku* can refer to any number of chrysanthemum species, from simple wild varieties to the elaborate horticultural varieties that are used in the grand annual displays held throughout Japan in the autumn. The *kiku* referred to in Heian-period poetry were low-mounded herbaceous plants that flowered late in the autumn season, even up until the time of the first frost.

The plant we now call *kiku* was introduced to Japan from China during the Nara period (710–784) as a horticultural and medicinal plant. Before then, there were chrysanthemum-like plants that were native to Japan with names such as *momoyo-gusa*, *uwagi*, and *kawara-yomogi*[109] that were probably among the broad group that are now generally referred to as *nogiku*, wild chrysanthemums or wild asters. In addition to those just mentioned, these *nogiku* include various species of the Kalimeris, Miyamayomena and Aster genera.

In China, chrysanthemums were associated with long life, a custom which transferred to Japan. Both *Genji Monogatari* and the *Murasaki Shikibu Nikki* make mention of the Festival of Chrysanthemums on the 9th day of the 9th month, called *chōyō no sechie*, during which courtiers would compose poems and drink *kikuzake* (chrysanthemum wine). The women of the court would dab their faces with cloth that had soaked up the dew from chrysanthemums in hopes of erasing the wrinkles of age and, if lucky, attaining a measure of longevity.[110] The first mention of *kiku* in Japan, in fact, is found in the 8th century record, *Kaifūsō*, which states that at a banquet given by Prince Nagaya-ō for an envoy from Silla, a poem was read that mentions chrysanthemums floating in *sake*.[111]

The varieties of chrysanthemum used for display in China were the result of crossbreeding Chrysanthemum indicum (*shimakangiku*, yellow flower) and Chrysanthemum zawadskii var. latilobum (*chōsen nogiku*, white flower or pale red).

In Gardens

That chrysanthemums were used in Heian-period gardens is not documented through archeological research but there is ample evidence in literature. *Genji Monogatari*, for instance, mentions chrysanthemums in gardens often. There is one well-known scene in which the Emperor Kiritsubo calls young Kaoru to the palace, hoping to have him take his daughter, the Second Princess, in marriage. A game of *go* is played, the Emperor loses and suggests that, as a prize of sorts, Kaoru should "take a flower." Kaoru picks a chrysanthemum, colored deeply by frost, from the garden and they exchange poems with hardly hidden meanings that use the chrysanthemum as an avatar for the obliquely proffered daughter.

In the *Murasaki Shikibu Nikki*, there is a scene in which a mansion is being prepared for an imperial visit.[112] Chrysanthemums that are especially uncommon are located and transplanted to the garden. There is a mixture of white ones, the color of which has deepened from the frost, and yellow ones. The author comments that this might help her stave off old age.

In Poetry

The *Man'yōshū*, which was compiled around 759, makes no mention of *kiku*. The poems in that anthology for the most part predate the importation of *kiku* from China but do mention other plants, such as *momoyo-gusa* and *uwagi*.

Kiku is used as a *makura-kotoba* in the form of *kiku no hana*, flowers of the chrysanthemum, which links to words such as the homonym *kiku* (聞く), that means to listen. *Kiku* (the flower) is an indicator of the transience and brevity of life, as are certain other flowers like the *sakura* (cherry) and *asagao* (morning glory). When autumn nights grow cold, and frost settles on chrysanthemums, their color fades or shifts. White flowers suddenly take on a reddish blush. This shift in color is used in poems to represent all manner of changes in the human experience, an example of which is in the poem that follows from the *Kokinshū*.

Although yellow chrysanthemums may have been the preference in China, white chrysanthemums take the favored spot in Japanese poetry. The whiteness of the flower is often linked to other images of white things in a process of association that has been known since the Edo period as *mitate*, or "associative linking." Waves breaking white upon the shore, snow, and moonlight are three examples of such white things. The poem from *Senzai Wakashū* that follows is a good example of this *mitate*.

古今和歌集 280
　　紀貫之
　　人の家なりけるきくの花をうつしうゑたりけるをよめる

咲きそめし　宿しかはれば　菊の花　色さへにこそ　移ろひにけれ
saki someshi　yado shi kawareba　kiku no hana　iro sae ni koso　utsuroinikere

　　Kokin Wakashū 280
　　　　Ki no Tsurayuki
　　　　A poem written upon moving a chrysanthemum from
another person's garden

　　　I took a chrysanthemum
　　　　　from a garden
　　　　　　　where it had begun to bloom
　　　Why on earth did I do that?
　　　　　even its color has started to fade

千載和歌集　347
　　内大臣
　　月照菊花といへる心をよみ侍りける

白菊の　葉におく露に　やどらずは　花とぞ見まじ　てらす月かげ
shiragiku no　ha ni oku tsuyu ni　yadorazu wa　hana to zo mimaji　terasu tsukikage

　　Senzai Wakashū 347
　　　　The Minister of the Interior
　　　　Written upon seeing moonlight on chrysanthemum

　　　If they hadn't gotten caught
　　　　　in those shiny pearls of dew
　　　　　　　resting on the white chrysanthemum's leaves
　　　I wouldn't have thought them flowers
　　　　　these glimmering moonbeams

Koke 苔 蘚 蘿 Moss

The Element

Moss needs no introduction — most people will be familiar with the low-growing groundcover that carpets the ground, stones, and trees alike. Mosses are an ancient plant, revealed in their simple structure. They have no flowers, or seeds (only spores), no vascular system for moving fluids around to different parts of the plant, and no fully developed root system. They typically prefer areas that are shaded, and moisture is a must. The leaves are small and thin and lack a waxy cuticle that would restrict the loss of water from the plant. They also need water for their spores to be able to move inside the plant for fertilization. The climate of Japan — an archipelago surrounded by tempering ocean currents and bathed by copious amounts of annual precipitation — is the perfect environment for the growth of mosses. Certainly in the central regions of Japan, where the Heian capital lay, if one clears a patch of bare ground and keeps it free from weeds, within a season or two a blush of new moss will surely cover the soil. The environment is that friendly to its growth. The flip side of this is that anything shaded and uncared for — whether it be a fence or a thatch roof — will soon begin to moss over.

There are many varieties of moss in Japan and it is impossible to determine for certain which ones were being referred to in Heian-period poetry, or grown in the gardens of that time, but a few of the most likely types are these: *kosugigoke* (小杉苔, Pogonatum inflexum); *seitaka sugigoke* (背高杉苔, Pogonatum japonicum); *uma sugigoke* (馬杉苔) or simply *sugigoke* (杉苔, Polytrichum commune); *ōsugigoke* (大杉苔, Polytrichum formosum); and *zenigoke* (銭苔, Marchantia polymorpha).

KAKITSUBATA

kakitsubata

nitsurau kimi wo

yukurinaku

omoiidetsutsu

nagekitsuru kamo

Man'yōshū 2521

IRIS

Ah sweet iris

your face flushed pink

Unexpectedly

I remember you

and sigh

We know that moss was used in gardens in the Heian period for several reasons. The *Sakuteiki* mentions *koke* twice. The first is in its instructions for making Meadow Style Island (*nojima*, 野島), where it suggests the use of moss in this way: "To make the Meadow Style island, build several low earth-berms traversing back and forth, and here and there, set some stones so that just their tops are visible above the ground. Plant autumnal grasses and, in the remaining open areas, plant moss and such." [113] Further on there is an admonishment against using stones that tumble down from mountain tops because their positioning has become "unnatural." Moss is described in this context as a modifying element.

> According to a man of the Sung Dynasty, stones taken from mountains or riverbanks have in fact tumbled down to the base of a mountain or valley floor from above, and in doing so the head and base of the stone have become reversed. Some are upright while others lie flat. Still, over time they will change color and become overgrown with moss. This weathering is not the work of man. Because the stones have weathered naturally, they can be set or laid in the garden as they are found in nature without impediment. [114]

There are many references to *koke* in *Genji Monogatari*, some in the forest in the wild, but also many in gardens. One interesting example, which is not in a garden but rather in a residence hall, is in the Otome chapter in which a kind of *bonsai* is described. A lid from a box acting as a tray has been spread with moss, some small craggy stones placed on the moss as miniature boulders, and a small Japanese white pine, *goyō matsu*, planted to evoke the image of a landscape. [115] Though not in a garden, we see that moss was used as part of the artistic life of the courtiers. At the very beginning of the Kochō chapter, we find a description of a boating party in the garden. On the isle in the lake were groves of trees beneath which spread out richly colored carpets of moss.[116] In the same section is a note that at the bottom of the steps that led down from one of the halls into the garden, in the part of the garden known as the "near garden," *omae no niwa*, there was moss. Genji orders his musicians to gather there, *on the moss*.[117] In the Kagerō chapter is a scene in which tragic Kaoru, Genji's purported son, visits the Uji residence of his deceased lover and, not wanting to enter the house, decides to sit down on the moss in the garden.[118] These last two entries are interesting because in modern-day gardens, according to modern-day customs, people rarely sit on moss the way people sit on lawns in Western gardens, but it seems in the Heian period people were comfortable with doing just that.

In Poetry

In Heian-period literature, *koke* is described in several ways. Often it is simply mentioned because it is green and lovely to look at. There are, however, other symbolic uses of *koke*. The first, and most common, is to use *koke* or the expression *koke ou*, or *koke musu*, both of which mean "covered in moss," to express the passage of time.[119] The idea is that things that have moss on them have been around for a while and, as such, have an aura of antiquity and permanence. This is often linked to words of praise, as in *Kokin Wakashū* 343 that wishes blessing on the king to "live thousands of years until boulders are covered with moss."[120] However, because *koke* will grow over things that are not cared for or maintained properly, it has also become linked, in almost the opposite way, with images of abandonment and dishevelment. In *Makura no Sōshi* we find a description of a scene in the west of the capital where the city was particularly run down. "The fences are all broken and everything covered with moss," the speaker says.[121] So *koke* is, at once, a symbol of longevity and of degeneration.

Koke is also used as a symbol to describe places that are pure and clean, quiet places that are sequestered from the human activity of cities and villages. In this light, it is naturally also linked to hermits and their hermitages. An expression that exemplifies this is *koke no koromo*, or *kokegoromo*, which translates as "robes of moss," and refers to both a luxurious carpet of moss and the robes of a Buddhist priest or hermit. Similar expressions are *koke no iori*, a mossy arbor, referring to the ancient dwelling of a mountain hermit, and *koke no makura*, a pillow of moss, that implies how close to nature a hermit is, and how simple and severe his life, that he would sleep outdoors, resting his head on moss-covered stones.

The last way that moss is used symbolically in poetry is in the expression *koke no shita*, under the moss, which refers to death, the dead, or the world of the dead.

千載和歌集　1107
　　仁和寺法親王守覺
　　高野にまうで侍りける時山路にてよみ侍りける

跡たえて　世をのがるべき　道なれや　岩さへ苔の　衣着てけり
atotaete　yo wo nogarubeki　michi nare ya　iwa sae koke no　koromo kitekeri

　　Senzai Wakashū 1107
　　　　Cloistered Prince Shukaku Hosshinnō of Ninnaji Temple
　　　　Composed while traveling along the mountain path to
　　Kōya Temple

　　　Leaving not even a trace
　　　　　we walk away from the world of men
　　　　　　　along this mountain path
　　　That must be why even the boulders here
　　　　　wear the hermit's mossy robes

万葉集 228
　　河辺宮人
　　姫島の松原に娘子の屍を見て、悲嘆しびて作る歌

妹が名は　千代に流れむ　姫島の　小松がうれに　苔生すまでに
imo ga na wa　chiyo ni nagaremu　himeshima no　komatsu ga ure ni　koke musu made ni

　　Man'yōshū 228
　　　　Kawabe Miyabito
　　　　Composed in sorrow after finding a girl's body in the pine
　　forest of Himeshima Island

　　　This young girl's name shall
　　　　　flow on for a thousand years
　　　Until these young pines
　　　　　of Maiden Island
　　　　　　　are old and thick with moss

Matsu 松 Pine

The Element

Matsu refers to any pine tree. Pines grow quickly and establish themselves in relatively poor soil, so they are found in natural groves in places as diverse as sandy shores along the sea and craggy bluffs in the mountains.

As far as which species of pine tree was being referred to in Heian-period poetry, it is difficult to know with certainty. Usually only the term *matsu* was used, or *komatsu*, which simply means small pine. The two most likely choices would be the Japanese black pine (Pinus thunbergii), which is typically found along shorelines, and the Japanese red pine (Pinus densiflora), which is usually associated with the mountains. One pine that is mentioned by name is the *goyō-matsu*, the Japanese white pine, which is, as the name states literally, a five-needled pine.

In Gardens

There is an overwhelming amount of evidence that pines were used in gardens. Archeological digs of Heian-period gardens have uncovered pine cones as well as needles of the Japanese red pine and Japanese black pine. The *Sakuteiki* mentions pines often. It suggests using them to create a Rocky Shore Isle by planting them between rough stones set on the edge of the pond. The trees, it says, should be old, even if not tall, nicely formed, and lush with green needles.[122] Later on it notes that pines were appropriate on islands where they should be planted along with willows.[123]

In both *Genji Monogatari* and *Makura no Sōshi* we find mentioned wisteria vines growing up pine trees and how beautiful they look, the bright purple, often fragrant flowers cascading down along the dark green needles. In Sei Shōnagon's list of "Things that Recall the Past but No Longer Have a

Purpose" she includes a withered pine strangled by a wisteria vine revealing not only that wisteria vines grow on pines but, left unchecked, they would eventually smother them.[124] In the *Eiga Monogatari*, which describes the life and times of Fujiwara no Michinaga, pines are mentioned as growing in gardens. One section tells how the Tsuchimikado mansion burned to the ground, taking with it all the ivy-covered pine trees and other old trees that grew on the islands in the pond and hills of the garden. It records that Michinaga felt that, although the house could be replaced (even if it was a splendid house), the old trees were irreplaceable.[125]

Depending on the scene in various stories, pine trees are mentioned either as being young/small or ancient/large. In the first case, the pines are symbols of virility, and in the second, of endurance. It is in this second light that we find Sei Shōnagon putting pine trees in her list of "Things That Ought to be Large."[126] Old pines in gardens are mentioned in other Heian-period texts as well. A compilation of Chinese-style poems made for Emperor Saga in 818, the *Bunka Shūreishū*, mentions "old pines" in the imperial garden, Shinsen'en, and *Shoku Nihon Kōki*, compiled in 869, has a record for 842 about the imperial-palace-turned-imperial-villa known as Reizei'in (also Reinen'in), that mentions that in the hills near the Fishing Pavilion there was a pine tree of about 5 meters (16 feet) in height.[127]

In Poetry

The pine is the king of trees when it comes to poetic usage. It appears countless times and in many forms. The word, *matsu*, might show up by itself, but as likely as not it will appear as part of a compound word, for instance, *hama-matsu*, beach-pine; *iso-matsu*, coastal pine; *yama-matsu*, mountain pine; *shima-matsu*, island pine; *waka-matsu*, young pine; *ko-matsu*, small pine (or young pine); *chiyo-matsu*, ancient pine; *matsu-kaze*, pine breeze; or *matsu-kage*, pine shadows.

Pine trees are also linked to images of sadness. This is epitomized by the chapter in *Genji Monogatari* called Matsukaze, the Wind in the Pines. One scene in that chapter describes the villa at Ōi at which the Akashi lady waits in a state of lonely melancholy far from home. She plays her *kin*, a Japanese harp, and the sound of the wind in the pines weaves its way through the music, adding to the melancholy of the scene.[128]

Because pines are evergreen trees (perhaps the best known evergreen tree, and thus representative) they are symbolic of eternal vigor or long life. This is evident in the poetic expressions such as *chiyo-matsu*, the thousand-year pine, and *tokiwanaru matsu*, the pine like an everlasting-stone.

The classic poetic relationship, so well known as to be considered almost a cliché, is between the two homonyms: *matsu*, a noun meaning "pine tree" and *matsu*, a verb meaning "to wait." This is also the only Japanese poetic device based on homonyms that works in English as well, since one can say "pining for one's lover." The image of pines is used in poems to evoke the sentiment of unrequited love, or of lovers waiting to be reunited with each other. The etymology of this connection is thought to be that the pine tree — considered to be a sort of a lighting rod for heavenly beings — was where people would wait and pray for the gods to descend from heaven.

古今和歌集 490

夕月夜　さすや岡部の　松の葉の　いつともわかぬ　恋もするかな
yūzukuyo　sasu ya okabe no　matsu no ha no　itsu tomo wakanu　koi mo suru kana

Kokin Wakashū 490

The pale moonlight
    spreads gently across the waiting
        pines of Okabe,
Evergreen   everlasting
    no less my heart's desire

万葉集　　2486

千沼の海の　浜辺の小松　根深めて　我恋ひ渡る　人の児故に
chinu no umi no　hama-he no komatsu　nefukamete　are koi wataru　hito no ko yue ni

Man'yōshū 2486

The young pines
    that grow along the shores of the Chinu Sea
        have gnarly roots
that tangle like my thoughts
    for someone else's lover

Momiji 紅葉 Japanese Maple

The Element

It is hard to define specifically what plant the word *momiji* refers to. In general the word is used to refer to "autumn colors" and so is a catch-all expression for any plant that has leaves that color richly in the fall. *Momiji* is the noun form of the classical Japanese verb, *momizu*, that means to turn colors in autumn, which may in turn derive from the verb *momu,* meaning "to rub or knead," because of the deep scarlet dye that can be extracted from safflowers (*beni-hana*) by rubbing them. Since the Heian period, *momiji* has been written with the two characters meaning scarlet leaves (紅葉), although in older texts, such as the *Man'yōshū*, *momiji* was commonly written with characters meaning golden leaves (黄葉). That being so, the word *momiji* as used in poems, or in Heian-period literature that describes gardens, could refer to anything from a deciduous tree such as Japanese maple or birch to shrubs with brilliant fall color, like the *dōdan tsutsuji* (Enkianthus perulatus).

Nowadays, the word *momiji* is used, almost exclusively, to indicate the Japanese maple. Maples are also often referred to with the overarching term, *kaede*, which is a shortened version of *kaerude*, or frog's hand, because the leaf of the Japanese maple tree looks so much like the webbed fingers of a frog. With regard to *kaede*, it is very possible that the species used in Heian-period gardens were the same as those still used today in Japanese gardens, in which case they would have been one or several of the following: *iroha momiji* (Japanese maple; Acer palmatum), *hauchiwa-kaede* (Fullmoon maple; Acer japonicum), and the *yama momiji* (Matsumurae maple; Acer amoenum var. matsumurae).

The seeds of a *kaede* (Acer) species have been found in the soil of archeological digs at Heian-period garden sites. The *Sakuteiki*, too, mentions both the words *momiji* and *kaede*. *Momiji* (i.e., trees with fall colors), it suggests, should be planted in the western part of a garden as opposed to flowering trees, which should be planted on the eastern side. This knowledge it attributes to the proverbial "Men of Old," in other words, common wisdom passed down through the ages. *Kaede*, according to the *Sakuteiki*, are well suited to be used near the Fishing Pavilion (*tsuridono*) built near or over a garden pond, designed to be cool in summer. The *Sakuteiki* says that trees such as the *kaede*, that will give cooling shade in summer, should be used there.[129]

In *Genji Monogatari*, the word *kaede* shows up only twice: once in a scene in which a maple (*kaede*) and an oak (*kashiwagi*) are entwined, and in another in which it is also described as being in the company of oaks in the garden. In both cases the leaves of the trees are green and fresh, so, while this shows that *kaede* were used in gardens, at least in this story, they are not necessarily linked to autumn. The word *momiji*, however, appears nearly sixty times in *Genji Monogatari*, always of course as part of an autumn scene. The classic scene of autumn gardens comes in the Otome chapter when Genji builds a palace for himself and the four important women in his life on a large property he owns on Rokujō Street. Each woman has her own apartment facing onto a separate garden. Murasaki no Ue, with Genji, is in the southeast (spring), Akikonomu in the southwest (autumn), Lady Akashi in the northwest (winter), and Hanachirusato in the northeast (summer). Akikonomu, whose name means Lover of Autumn, has a garden that favors the autumn season including the planting of many trees that would have rich autumn colors, in other words, *momiji*.[130]

In Poetry

Naturally, *momiji* is used in poems as an indicator of the autumn season. Like other autumn words, it is often connected to expressions of wind (*kaze*), dew (*tsuyu*), and cold, drizzling rain (*shigure*).

The word *momiji*, is used as a *makura-kotoba* in the form of *momijiba no*, leaves of autumn colors. It links to words such as *utsuru* (to change), *sugu* (to pass), and *ake* (red color; *aka*). The first two are often connected in poetry to a mention of a person's death as in the poem from the *Man'yōshū* presented below. Please note that in pre-Heian period Japanese, such as that of the *Man'yōshū*, the word *momiji* was pronounced *momichi*.

万葉集　47
　　軽皇子、安騎の野に宿る時に、柿本朝臣人麻呂の作る歌

ま草刈る　荒野にはあれど　黄葉の　過ぎにし君が　形見とそ来し
ma kusa karu　arano ni wa aredo　momichi ba no　suginishi kimi ga　katami to so koshi

> *Man'yōshū* 47
> 　　Kakinomoto no Hitomaro
> 　　When Prince Karu lodged on the Fields of Akino
>
> Although this is but a wild moor
> 　　where we come only to harvest the rich grasses
> 　　　　we gather now in memory
> The brocade of autumn colors
> 　　and our Prince, now passed[131]

千載和歌集　369
　　藤原公重朝臣
　　近衛院の御時、禁庭落葉といへる心をよめる

庭のおもに　ちりてつもれる　もみぢ葉は　九重にしく　にしきなりけり
niwa no mo ni　chirite tsumoreru　momijiba wa　kokonoe ni shiku　nishiki narikeri

> *Senzai Wakashū* 369
> 　　Fujiwara no Kinshige
> 　　On Autumn leaves scattering in the garden at the time of
> Retired Emperor Konoe[132]
>
> The autumn leaves
> 　　scatter and gather
> 　　　　in the palace garden
> Weaving golden brocades
> 　　nine layers deep

Mushi 虫 Insects

As with any country, Japan abounds with insects. The people of the Japanese court in the Heian period seemed to have had a particular affection for various insects, filling their poetry and diaries with mentions of them. There was even a folk-tale, written down at the end of the Heian period called *Mushi Mezuru Himegimi, The Princess who Loved Insects*, about a young princess who was so taken with insects of all forms that she neglected her social/courtly duties. The people of the Heian court did not love all insects of course. The ones that garner the most attention are the crickets (*suzumushi* and *matsumushi*), the cicada (*semi* or *higurashi*), and the firefly (*hotaru*). Many more are mentioned. Sei Shōnagon puts a whole list of them in her *Makura no Sōshi*. Some she thinks on pleasantly, like the *natsu-mushi*, literally "summer bug," which could include fireflies, cicadas, or moths, and others not so pleasantly, like the *hae*, or common fly. It's interesting that she, and other writers and poets of Japan's classical period, seemed to hold a fancy for moths but have little interest in butterflies. The insects on her list, and found elsewhere in classical literature, include the cricket, cicada, and firefly mentioned above, as well as the grasshopper, *kirigirisu* (now called *kōrogi*), and *hataori* (now called *kirigirisu*); mayfly, *kagerō*; ant, *ari*; bagworm, *minomushi*; click beetle, *nukazukimushi* (now called *kometsukimushi*); and spider, *kumo*.[133] *Mushi* could also include worms. The princess in *Mushi Mezuru Himegimi*, for instance, particularly liked caterpillars. In this section, we will concentrate on two insects with well-known cries: crickets and cicadas.

The two most commonly found crickets in Heian-period literature are the *suzumushi* and the *matsumushi*. Precisely which crickets these were is not proven definitively but it is thought that the modern-day *suzumushi* was the Heian-period *matsumushi* and vice versa. If this is correct, then the Heian-period *suzumushi* was Xenogryllus marmoratus and the Heian-period *matsumushi* was Homoeogryllus japonicus. As with crickets elsewhere, the *suzumushi* and the *matsumushi*, whatever their scientific names really were, are typically found in grassy meadows, and begin to cry as the nights cool in autumn.

There are many types of cicadas in Japan, which dig their way out of the ground, climb trees to metamorphose into their winged, adult form, and fill the air with their cries. In classical literature these were almost always referred to with the generic word, *semi*, or the specific name, *higurashi*. If the *higurashi* of the Heian period was the same cicada as it is today, it would have been Tanna japonensis.

In Gardens

As to whether these insects — the crickets and cicadas — were actually to be found in gardens in the Heian period, the answer is, as mentioned before with fireflies, try keeping them out. Time and time again, in *Genji Monogatari* and other stories, the characters listen to the sad chirping of crickets in the autumn garden and lament the pathos of life. Not nearly as often as crickets, but still more than just once or twice, the summer garden is punctuated by the shrill cry of the cicada. Many times, in fact, the original text simply says *mushi*, insect, and one is left to guess by the season and the mood what that insect might be.

What is interesting about crickets, though, is that although they certainly found their way into gardens naturally, they were also intentionally caught and introduced into gardens for their sound. There was in the Heian period a game played called *mushi-awase*, a variant of the general game, *mono-awase*, or comparison contest, in which a person's discernment was tested by presenting a group of things from which a selection was to be made. For *mushi-awase*, different types of insects would be caught, put in cages, and made to sing so that the teams could try to identify them. Or, once identified, the team would need to compose a poem on the theme of that insect on the spot. In order to collect enough specimens, people went out to the meadows to engage in *mushi-erabi*, which literally means selecting insects but in reality meant simply catching them. After the contests were finished, people may have kept the insects in cages. In the Nowaki chapter of *Genji Monogatari*, for instance, there is a scene in which page girls feed dew from the garden to crickets they keep in cages.[134] There is also another scene, this one in the aptly named Suzumushi chapter, that reveals that crickets, both *suzumushi* and *matsumushi*, were intentionally collected from wild moors and released into autumn gardens to heighten the seasonal atmosphere.[135]

In Poetry

As we have seen, in poetry, as in reality, crickets are indicators of autumn while cicadas typically mark the height of summer. So the first reason these insects are used in poetry is as a seasonal marker, but there are some other symbolic uses as well. Crickets are naturally associated with wild grassy moors and meadows, and their crying, while not similar to human crying, is still evocative of sadness. Dew on the grasses becomes a metaphor for tears, so all of these things — autumn, wild meadows, wind-blown grasses, dew, and the fading cries of crickets as the season wanes — add up to evoke a feeling of melancholy and a lamentation on the quick passage of life. In addition, with relation to pine crickets, *matsumushi*, as was described in the section on pine trees, the word *matsu* also means "to wait" and that double meaning is used in poems about the insect as well as the tree.

Cicadas, on the other hand, being a summer insect, and incredibly loud and incessant in their crying, do not naturally evoke an image of sadness. Their sheer wings and appearance in summer were poetically linked so that poems that mention cicadas might flow naturally into the image of light summer clothes. The name of one of the species of *semi*, the *higurashi*, meaning "bringing on the dusk," links the image of cicadas with sunset. And, the predilection of the Heian culture to find pathos in anything, was able to find it in the cicada too. Or, rather, not in the cicada, but in the husk it leaves clinging to trees when its larva molts and continues up the tree in a new form. This dry shell — exactly the size and shape of a cicada larva but empty — was called *utsusemi* (空蝉), the empty cicada. Written with different characters, *utsusemi* (現身) means "a living person," "people of this world," or, in the expression *utsusemi no yo*, "this mortal world." As such, the expression *utsusemi no* became a *makura-kotoba* used in poems to link to *hito* (people), *yo* (the world), *mi* (the body), and *inochi* (life).

古今和歌集　715
　　紀友則
　　寛平御時后の宮の歌合の歌

蟬の声　きけばかなしな　夏衣　うすくや人の　ならむと思へば
semi no koe　kikeba kanashi na　natsugoromo　usuku ya hito no　naramu to omoeba

> *Kokin Wakashū* 715
> 　　Ki no Tomonori
> 　　Composed at the poetic contest of the Empress in the era
> of Kanpyō
>
> 　　Hearing the cicada's cry
> 　　　　I fill with sadness
> 　　　　　　reflecting on how quickly
> 　　Your feelings for me
> 　　　　will wear as thin as summer clothes

後撰和歌集　1287
　　左大臣
　　昔を思ひ出でゝむら子の内侍につかはしける

鈴虫に　劣らぬ音こそ　泣かれけれ　昔の秋を　思やりつゝ
suzumushi ni　otoranu ne koso　nakarekere　mukashi no aki wo　omoiyari tsutsu

> *Gosen Wakashū* 1287
> 　　Minister of the Left
> 　　Thinking over the past, I sent this to the Palace Attendant,
> Mura no ko.
>
> 　　I just sit and weep
> 　　　　a sound more miserable
> 　　　　　　than bell crickets crying
> 　　Thinking back　　over and over
> 　　　　that autumn so long ago

Nadeshiko 撫子 *Dianthus*

Nadeshiko is a perennial flower found in meadows, along riverbanks, and on sandy seashores. It grows between 30 and 60 centimeters (1 to 2 feet) in height and flowers in various shades of pink from the end of summer into autumn. It is a species of Dianthus but, as with many other plants, it is not precisely clear which species was referred by the Heian-period writers. The most likely choice is a variety called *kawara-nadeshiko*, Dianthus superbus var. longicalycinus, which is known as fringed pink in English, or just pink, but there are other species that are also native to Japan, such as *hama-nadeshiko*, Dianthus japonicus, that are possibilities. In fact, *nadeshiko* may refer to any Dianthus with characteristics similar to those described above.

In addition to varieties that are native to Japan, at some point during the Heian period, another species, Dianthus chinensis, was imported from China. The Japanese referred to this as *sekichiku*, literally, "stone bamboo." The native flowers were also called *yamato-nadeshiko* and those from China *kara-nadeshiko*, Yamato being the name of an ancient Japanese kingdom and Kara being the Japanese name for the Tang dynasty.

In Gardens

Nadeshiko appear often enough in literature to make clear that they were well-known flowers among the Heian courtiers. In *Genji Monogatari*, they are mentioned over twenty times, often in such a way that it is clear they were planted in a garden — not simply in the wild — and, furthermore, in a part of the garden that is easily seen from the rooms of the residence. This part of the garden was usually called the *omae*, the near garden, and was the place where people would plant those plants they wanted to appreciate most closely. The flowers are often described as being intermingled with a fence or hedge, *magaki*, which probably means they were planted in clumps along the bottom of an open-weave fence and could be seen growing through the fence itself. The season of the scenes is either the height of summer — in the Maboroshi chapter cicadas are crying and the lotuses in the pond are in full bloom — or summer passing into autumn, as in the Nowaki chapter which describes page girls in the garden after an autumn typhoon has passed through, picking pinks for the Empress. At his Rokujō palace, in which Genji builds four gardens in four sections of his estate for four women, each of which has a seasonal theme, he plants *nadeshiko* for Hanachirusato in the northeastern garden, which is the garden designed for summer, mixed in with roses and peonies.[136]

In Poetry

In poetry, *nadeshiko* is usually an indicator of the summer season. That said, the other name for *nadeshiko*, *tokonatsu*, which means "endless summer," makes reference to the fact that the blooms last past the end of summer and into autumn. And, *nadeshiko* is on the list of the Seven Flowers of Autumn along with *hagi*, *obana* (*susuki*), *kuzu*, *ominaeshi*, *fujibakama*, and *kikyō* (or *asagao*, depending on the era). So, *nadeshiko* can be seen as a cross-over plant related to both summer and autumn.

One of the distinctive aspects of poems about *nadeshiko* in the *Man'yōshū* is that almost all of them are poems in which the author is not only known (whereas many of the poems are anonymous) but is also of high social standing. Apparently *nadeshiko* were favored by courtiers from ancient times. The name, *nadeshiko*, is written with two characters that mean "to pet" and "a child" — in other words an adorable or lovable child (literally, "the child I love"). The expression, *yamato-nadeshiko*, therefore, refers not only to the native flower, but the image of an idealized Japanese woman who represents all of the virtues and beauties of her time.

拾遺和歌集　132
　　伊勢
　　家に咲きて侍りける撫子を人のがり遣はしける

いづこにも　咲きはすらめど　我が宿の　山と撫子　誰に見せまし
izuko nimo　saki wa suramedo　waga yado no　yamato nadeshiko　tare ni misemashi

　　Shūi Wakashū 132
　　　　Ise
　　　　I sent the lovely pink blooming in my garden to someone

　　Pinks might bloom
　　　　wherever they are sent
　　　　　　but this lovely flower　　child of my heart
　　Grown of my own home —
　　　　who should I show her to but you

　　　　　　　　☙　　　　❧

古今和歌集　167
　　みつね
　　隣より常夏の花をこひにおこせたりければ、惜しみてこの歌をよみて
つかはしける

塵をだに　すゑじとぞ思ふ　咲きしより　妹とわが寝る　とこなつの花
chiri wo dani　sueji to zo mou　sakishi yori　imo to waga nuru　tokonatsu no hana

　　Kokin Wakashū 167
　　　　Mitsune
　　　　Composed and sent in regret to a neighbor who had asked
　　for my *tokonatsu* flower

　　　I have not let even a speck
　　　　　of this world's dust touch them
　　　Since they first flowered
　　　　　these lovely pinks　　have been the cherished bed
　　　　　　　which cradles my wife and me

160

No 野 Meadow

The Element

The word *no* means meadow in Japanese and refers to the same thing it would anywhere else — a relatively open expanse of land that is not too steep (not a mountainside) and is covered in grasses, perennials, and shrubs, rather than a forest of trees. Ancient texts, such as the *Kojiki, Records of Ancient Matters*, use the paired expressions of "mountains and meadows" to mean all of the natural world, overseen by two deities, one for the mountains and one for the plains.[137] The mountains, *yama*, would be associated more closely with wild nature, and the plains or meadows, *no*, would be places of human activity; places where people would hunt small game, collect grasses for use as thatch, and make vegetable patches by burning off grass and trees. As such, the image of the meadow took on certain complex meanings, juxtaposing a place of human work with that of wild nature — the everyday world with the world of a higher spiritual plane. Literature has left us with a long list of meadows that were famous: among them, Takano, Kumano, Sagano, Nagano, Ueno, Murasakino, Musashino, and Yoshino.

In Gardens

Meadows were intentionally created in Heian-period gardens by designers who were trying to capture the beauty of the wild meadow. Of course, a life-sized meadow was not feasible on a Heian-period courtier's property, the largest of which was typically only one *chō* or 120 meters by 120 meters in size (14,400 square meters, 1.44 hectares, or about 3.5 acres). Of this, only a quarter, at most, was devoted to the garden of which half may have been taken up by a large central pond, and half of the remaining by hillocks and such, leaving less than 1,000 square meters (a quarter of an acre) for a meadow. Since most gardens were smaller than this, it was most likely that the average meadow in a garden was in fact a symbolic representation of the wild form, with some of the attributes but not the true size.

In *Genji Monogatari*, there are several instances in which wild meadow-like aspects of the gardens are described — even some scenes that capture the intentional creation of meadow landscapes in gardens. In the Otome chapter, Prince Genji builds a large garden at his Rokujō palace for himself and four women — each woman having her own quadrant of the garden focused on a different season. The autumn garden features maple trees, of course, but also a meadow scene planted with perennials that will be at their best in autumn. Likewise, in the Suzumushi chapter, Genji reworks a garden in the image of a wild meadow, going so far as to release crickets into it to capture the beautifully lonely quality of an autumn meadow. Sei Shōnagon, in *Makura no Sōshi*, mentions that wild meadows look nice because of the *susuki*, miscanthus grasses, and, elsewhere in the book, puts the autumn meadow on her list of things that are poignant or emotionally touching, *awarenaru mono*.[138]

The *Sakuteiki* has many comments about meadows and how to create them in the garden. The term used in the *Sakuteiki* was *nosuji* (野筋), but the word *nosuji* was at that time, and is still today, not a common expression, used primarily in gardening manuals or in poems that refer to gardens.[139] To create a meadow, the *Sakuteiki* suggests, one should "build several low earth-berms traversing back and forth, and here and there, set some stones so that just their tops are visible above the ground. Plant autumnal grasses and, in the remaining open areas, plant moss and such."[140] There are also comments about what kind of plants would be best to use. It suggests that the "Meadow scenes in the vicinity of a Garden Stream should not be planted with plants that will grow thick and full. Rather, plants like Chinese bellflower, patrinia, burnet, and plantain lily should be planted."[141]

In Poetry

In poetry, the meadow itself is usually not the subject of the poem. Instead, the subject will be one of the many aspects of nature that one can find in meadows. *Susuki*, for instance, which is a tall miscanthus grass and is a seasonal marker for autumn and often described as being full and beautiful. Sedges, such as *asaji* and *suge*, grow thickly, marking the passage of time. Dew may coat those grasses with heavy pearls. Stags bellow their forlorn cry, often near bush clover, *hagi*, which is paired with the stag as a botanical representation of the deer's mate. The wind may hurl across the grasses, often a bitter cold wind. In fact, the expression *nowaki* (meadow splitter) refers to the powerful winds of autumn. Birds abound, often quail (*uzura*) and pheasants (*kiji*), as do insects, crickets mainly, whose chirping captures the imagination of the poet. Although in the *Man'yōshū* many poems about *no* are set in spring, by the Heian period, autumn became the de facto season related to meadows. All in all, the meadow is either a place of reflection — thinking back on the memory of a great king or a distant lover — or a place of severity — cold, exposed, a setting through which to express emotional turmoil.

千載和歌集　　270
　　小辨（小弁）
　　住み侍りける山里をしばしほかに侍りて帰りたりけるに前栽のいた
くしをれたりければよめる

宿かれて　幾日もあらぬに　鹿のなく　秋の野べとも　なりにけるかな
yado karete　ikuka mo aranu ni　shika no naku　aki no nobe tomo　narinikeru kana

　　Senzai Wakashū 270
　　Shōben
　　Composed after having been away from my mountain
　　village home for some time and returning to find the garden
　　plants all withered

　　I left my mountain home
　　　　and in just the time I was gone
　　　　　　I find it fading
　　The garden now a wild autumn meadow
　　　　pierced by the lonely stag's cry

万葉集　　227

天離る　鄙の荒野に　君を置きて　思ひつつあれば　生けるともなし
amazakaru　hina no arano ni　kimi wo okite　omoitsutsu areba　ikeru tomo nashi

　　Man'yōshū 227

　　On a wild moor
　　as distant and empty as the stars
　　　　I walked away from you
　　The memory rises — over and over
　　　　and I die a little each time

Numa 沼 Marsh, Wetland

The Element

A *numa* is any low-lying piece of ground where surface water collects naturally or where underground springs feed surface water. It is like a pond but more shallow (technically under 5 meters, 16 feet), typically muddy, and populated by various water plants, such as reeds (*ashi*, 葦), irises (*kakitsubata*, 杜若), sweet rush (*ayame*, 菖蒲), water lilies (*suiren*, 睡蓮), and algae (*mo*, 藻). Sometimes these pools of water are simply called *numa*, but they may also be referred to as *nu, numa-mizu, sawa*, or *sawa-ike*. In English, a *numa* could be called a swamp, bog, marsh, fen, or a wetland.

One distinctive feature of many *numa* is that, although water clearly flows into the marsh, there does not appear to be a clear way in which excess water flows out. It either seeps into the ground water system or trickles out in various directions. This feature has a poetic link as we shall see.

In Gardens

The existence of a *numa* in gardens is not mentioned in narrative literary works such as *Genji Monogatari* or *Makura no Sōshi*. It is mentioned, however, very specifically in the *Sakuteiki* in which it is called *numaike no yō*[142] or the Wetland Style of gardening.

> Stones are rarely used in designing the Wetland Style; rather, in a little inlet, one should plant some water plants, reeds, and irises. There is no need for an island, and only a glimpse of water should appear between the plants. In the Wetland Style, water from a small channel should gather in one place, and the point where water runs in and out of

the Wetland should not be clearly revealed. Water should simply appear from some hidden, unseen origin, and the surface of the water should appear high and full.[143]

In Poetry

As mentioned above, *numa* often have no clear point of outflow for the water. Poetically, this fact is used to represent the disconsolate feeling of being lost. Thus, the *makura-kotoba, numa mizu no,* links to *yukue mo naki,* having "nowhere to go." Likewise, the fact that the waters of a *numa* may be muddy, and its surface covered by water plants — in some cases entirely — has resulted in the *numa* becoming a poetic symbol for hidden things. In the era of the *Man'yōshū* this was referred to as *komorinu,* whereas in the Heian period the expression *kakurenu* became more common.[144]

万葉集　3022

行くへなみ　隠れる小沼の　下思に　我れぞ物思ふ　このころの間
yukue nami　komoreru onu no　shitamoi ni　ware zo monomou　kono koro no aida

Man'yōshū 3022

Anxious thoughts
　　　of my secret love
Swamp me these days
　　　pooling with no release — like the hidden waters
　　　　　of this little marsh

　　　　　　　　ʕ　　　ʔ

古今和歌集　661
　　紀友則
　　寛平御時后の宮の歌合の歌

紅の　色にはいでじ　隠れ沼の　下にかよひて　恋は死ぬとも
kurenai no　iro niwa ideji　kakurenu no　shita ni kayoite　koi wa shinu tomo

Kokin Wakashū 661
　　Ki no Tomonori
　　Composed at the time of the Emperor Kampyō for the
Poetry Contest held by the Empress

I'll not show my color —
　　a safflower flushing crimson
　　　but keep it close and hidden
Water flowing below the weedy marsh
　　a secret love — even unto death

MATSU

yūzukuyo
sasu ya okabe no
matsu no ha no
itsu tomo wakanu
koi mo suru kana

Kokin Wakashū 490

PINE

The pale moonlight
spreads gently across the waiting
pines of Okabe,
Evergreen   everlasting
no less my heart's desire

夕月夜しづや
閑見送の来る笑ひ

いつもやうぬ
折心すゝのに

Ominaeshi: 女郎花 Valerian

Ominaeshi is a perennial flower that grows in open meadows, reaching about one meter (3 feet) in height and setting many yellow flowers in late summer or early autumn. The botanical name is Patrinia scabiosaefolia, and there are several names in English: golden valerian, or just valerian, patrinia, golden lace, and maidenflower. The reason for the last name will become apparent shortly. Likewise, there are many ways to write *ominaeshi* in Japanese: 女郎花 is the most common but there are others such as 佳人部師 and 美人部師, or simply the kana script, をみなへし.

In Gardens

The *Sakuteiki* mentions the use of *ominaeshi* once, with regard to the creation of meadow scenes in the garden. It reads: "The Meadow scenes in the vicinity of a Garden Stream should not be planted with plants that will grow thick and full. Rather, plants like Chinese bellflower, patrinia, burnet, and plantain lily should be planted."[145] This connection to meadow landscapes coincides with both the ecology of the plant — that is where they are found in nature — and also the literary use of the plant in which it invariably was part of a meadow scene.

There are many instances of *ominaeshi* showing up in *Genji Monogatari*, but most of those are in poems that the characters are reciting to each other. There are at least two cases, however, in which *ominaeshi* is described in the garden, once in the Yadorigi chapter in which Kaoru plucks a morning glory, *asagao*, rich with dew from the garden but doesn't even notice the nearby maidenflowers, *ominaeshi*, and another in the Tenarai chapter in which a hedge/fence is described as having *ominaeshi*, *nadeshiko*, and *asagao* intermixed within it.[146]

In *Makura no Sōshi*, *ominaeshi* is mentioned as growing in a garden next to *hagi* bushes, both, unfortunately, crushed under limbs of trees that were blown over by a strong wind.[147] We also find *ominaeshi* mentioned in *Murasaki Shikibu Nikki* where the Regent, Fujiwara no Michinaga, plucks a large cluster of *ominaeshi* from where it bloomed near the south side of the garden bridge. He tosses the flower to Murasaki behind her screen and they exchange poems on the theme of *ominaeshi* and dew. This scene is repeated in the *Murasaki Shikibu Shū*.[148]

In Poetry

In poetry, *ominaeshi* is, as seen above, a symbolic marker of autumn and of meadows. It is also related to the image of women, especially beautiful women. Within the word *ominaeshi* is the sound *omina*, which can mean "beautiful maiden," and *eshi* or *heshi* means to overwhelm, thus an overwhelmingly attractive woman.[149] This is the reason that *ominaeshi* is sometimes referred to as the maidenflower. This relationship — that *ominaeshi* represents young women — is the most prevalent in poetry. These women are often beautiful and in some cases fickle, their love superficial or subject to whims. The flower can be used to evoke the image of "all those pretty young maids out there," often continuing to a protest of disinterest.

The use of *ominaeshi* and dew together is usually a metaphor for man and wife. The passage above, between Murasaki and the Regent (who were not, of course, man and wife), was done playfully with that understanding.

As a *makura-kotoba*, *ominaeshi* can link to the word *ou*, to be alive, and to *saku*, to flower, as well as to place names that contain the word *saki* (a homonym for flowering) such as Sakisawa and Sakino.[150]

古今和歌集　1016
　　僧正へんぜう

秋の野に　なまめき立てる　女郎花　あなかしかまし　花も一時
aki no no ni namameki tateru ominaeshi ana kashikamashi hana mo hitotoki

Kokin Wakashū 1016
　　The Honorable Priest Henjō

The maidenflowers stand
　　so beautiful　　so full of life
　　　　across the autumn field
Charming　　graceful　　and yet
　　flowers last but a moment

千載和歌集　251
　　大納言師頼
　　堀川院の御時百首の歌奉りける時よみ侍りける

露しげき　朝の原の　をみなへし　ひとゑだをらむ　袖はぬるとも
tsuyu shigeki ashita no hara no ominaeshi hitoeda oramu sode wa nuru tomo

Senzai Wakashū 251
　　Dainagon Moroyori, Chief Councilor of State
　　Composed at the time of the Cloistered Emperor
Horikawa, when I presented my set of 100 poems as an offering
to the Emperor

The maidenflowers
　　of the broad morning plain
　　　　hang thick with morning dew
I will break one off
　　even if it wets my sleeve

Sakaki 榊 Japanese Cleyera

Sakaki is an evergreen tree with glossy dark green leaves that grows to about 8 to 10 meters (25 to 33 feet) in height. Usually written 榊, the double characters meaning "virtuous tree" 賢木 are sometimes used instead. Because of its luxuriant green leaves, it has been used in religious ceremonies from ancient times as a symbol of eternal life or life energy. In Shintō rituals, a shrine priest will often carry a single, fan-like branch of *sakaki*, waving it quickly back and forth in the air to make a rustling sound as a symbolic act of cleansing. The plant called *sakaki* today is the Japanese cleyera, Cleyera japonica. Although it is likely this same plant was called *sakaki* and used in shrine rituals since ancient times, it is also possible that the word *sakaki* in fact referred to a number of glossy-leafed, evergreen plants that were used interchangeably in shrine rituals, such as the plants now called *hisakaki* (Eurya, Eurya japonica, 姫榊) and *shikimi* (Japanese star anise, Illicium religiosum, 樒).

The derivation of the name *sakaki* has several probable explanations, one being that it is related to *sakai-ki* (境木), the "border tree," and another being that it is related to *sakae-ki* (栄木), the "flourishing or luxuriant tree." The latter explanation, of course, relates to the dark green, glossy leaves of the tree and its symbol of richly flourishing life. The former, "border tree," refers to the fact that it was either planted as a hedge to define the border of a shrine or, more interestingly, that, because it was used in rituals in which the shrine priest was calling on the *kami*, or gods, it was seen as being on the border between "this world" and the "world of the *kami*."

There are many references to *sakaki* in classical literature from the *Kojiki* and *Nihon Shoki* onward. In those texts it is often referred to as *masakaki*, the true *sakaki*, which implies that, as mentioned above, there may have been several plants called *sakaki* and one, thought to be the best of all for ceremonial use, called *masakaki*. Sei Shōnagon, in a list of trees she comments on in her *Makura no Sōshi*, mentions how wonderful the *sakaki* looks at special events like shrine dances, *kagura*. This, she says, is because, of all the trees in the world, it is the *sakaki* that is presented before the gods.[151] So there are many instances in which *sakaki* appears in literature as a part of religious ceremonies but the only reference to *sakaki* in gardens comes in the *Sakuteiki*.

One of the aspects stressed in the *Sakuteiki* is the geomantic quality of gardens. In particular, the text points out what should and should not be done in the garden in certain directions as seen from the vantage point of the residence, which was generally situated in the center of the property with the garden laid out in front of it to the south. Since the *sakaki* was associated with rituals in which the gods were contacted, and thus considered a sacred plant, it was not to be used casually in a garden. The *Sakuteiki* simply states, "Planting a *sakaki* in the direction one usually faces should be avoided."[152]

In Poetry

In poetry, *sakaki* is not employed as a particular *makura-kotoba* or *kake-kotoba*. Instead, it appears in poems that are related to shrines, or the gods, or long life. Nowadays, in shrine ceremonies, in lieu of a *sakaki* branch, streamers of white paper folded into zigzag patterns, called *gohei*, are tied to a wooden stick and rustled through the air in the same sort of quick sweeping motion. In several of the oldest literary references, we find scenes in which strips of white mulberry cloth, written with the same character but pronounced *mitegura*, are tied to *sakaki* branches and used in a similar way.[153] So the imagery associated with *sakaki* are all religious and the plant was used in literature to bring out those associations.

神垣の　御室の山の　榊葉は　神のみ前に　茂りあひにけり

kamigaki no　mimuro no yama no　sakakiba wa　kami no mimae ni　shigeriainikeri

Kokin Wakashū 1074

The richly-leaved *sakaki* trees
that encircle the shrine
on sacred Mimuro mountain
These are surely meant for the gods
So abundant, thick, and dense

千載和歌集　1266
権大納言實國
廣田の社の歌合とて人々歌よみ侍りける時社頭雪といへる心をよみ
侍りける

をしなべて　雪の白木綿　掛けてけり　いづれ榊の　梢なるらむ

oshinabete　yuki no shirayū　kaketekeri　izure sakaki no　kozue naruramu

Senzai Wakashū 1266

Assistant Chief Councilor of State, Sanekuni
I composed this for a poetry contest at Hirota Shrine, in
which many people took part, on the theme of snows covering
the Shrine

From end to end
snow drapes the landscape　　like drifts
of white mulberry cloth
Which then are the tops
of the ever verdant sakaki

Sakura 桜 櫻 *Cherry*

The Element

Sakura is the name for the cherry tree. There are many varieties, especially nowadays after hundreds of years of horticultural development, but as a general rule, the cherry produces white or light pink blooms in early- to mid-spring. The flowers can be single or double and are often profuse.

Though certainly not exclusive to Japan, the cherry is one of the quintessential plants of Japan. All of the cherries are of the genus Prunus (as are other well-known trees such as plums and peaches), but it is not known precisely which cherries are being referred to in the literature of the Heian period. One thing, however, is without doubt. The cherry tree most associated with Japan these days — one that is planted in groves in every public park, and is found lining streets and riverbanks throughout Japan —is not that ancient tree. This modern cherry, known as *somei-yoshino* (Prunus yedoensis, 染井吉野), was developed as a horticultural variety in the late 1800s and although ubiquitous in Japan is not the historical plant of classical Japan. The cherry trees that show up in older texts were most likely mountain cherries, *yama-zakura*, Prunus serrulata.[154] One main difference between the *somei-yoshino* and the *yama-zakura* is that the new leaves of the latter unfold in spring just before flowering whereas the *somei-yoshino* blooms before leafing out. Because they are unobstructed, the flowers of the *somei-yoshino* are particularly spectacular but this would not have been the case for the cherries seen and recorded by the Heian-period courtiers. Those cherries would have had the mellower visual complexity of the *yama-zakura* which leaf and flower at the same time.

In the *Man'yōshū*, which represents periods that precede the Heian

176

period, the plum is a particular favorite of the intellectual poets, more so than the cherry. This is because it was newly imported from China and projected an attendant air of high culture and sophistication. By the Heian period, however, the native cherry had gained (or regained) its position as the preeminent flowering tree, revealed in part by its usage in poetry but also by the fact that sometime before the year 874 the prescribed planting of a plum in front of the main hall of the imperial palace, Shishinden, was replaced by a cherry. *Nihon Sandai Jitsuroku, The True History of Three Reigns of Japan*, has an entry for the 8ᵗʰ month of Jōgan 16 (874) that mentions a "cherry in front of Shishinden."[155]

In Gardens

We know from many sources that cherries were used in the gardens of the Heian period. Archeological research has found the seed pits of cherry species in Heian-period garden sites and literary evidence abounds. Toba-dono, the detached palace of Emperor Shirakawa and later Emperor Toba, is recorded as having had *yae-zakura*, or double flowering cherries, planted on its grounds.[156] Another interesting note about cherries in gardens is found in *Kanke Bunsō*, a late-9ᵗʰ-century record that mentions an imperial edict to replace a dead cherry tree by transplanting a tree from the mountains.[157]

In *Genji Monogatari*, cherries are often depicted in gardens. At Prince Genji's Rokujō palace, for instance, where he built four gardens for four women, each with a different seasonal theme, the southeastern garden — which featured spring plantings — included cherry trees. In the Maboroshi chapter, after the death of Murasaki no Ue for whom the garden was originally built, Genji reflects on how skillfully she had arranged the various types of cherries to feature them as they each came into bloom at slightly different times including single- and double-petalled varieties and a mountain variety called *kaba-zakura*.[158]

Cherries are also mentioned often in *Makura no Sōshi*. At one point the author muses fondly on how the autumn leaves of cherries and elms will make a carpet of gold in the garden. This is one of the rare comments that links cherries to the beauties of autumn rather than those of spring.[159] In both *Makura no Sōshi* and *Murasaki Shikibu Shū*, cherries are also mentioned as having been used in flower arrangements. It would seem branches from flowering trees were cut off and displayed in large vases, at least one of which was a celadon-glazed ceramic vase.[160]

In Poetry

It goes without saying that in poetry, cherries were an indicator of spring and also depicted by poets who were reveling in the simple beauty of the natural world. At times the word *sakura* was used, at others simply *hana*, or flower, because often one needed to say no more than flower to make the reader know one meant cherry. Beyond these, however, there are two consistent ways that cherries were used symbolically

The first is related to beauty. Cherries were often used to mean a beautiful woman in the same way as other flowers, such as the *ominaeshi*.

The second is ephemerality. After the a cherry tree has bloomed for a few days, if there is particularly warm weather or a good rain, or especially when both happen together, the petals will drop, drifting to the ground in cascades resembling snowfall. This brief existence — so apparently full of life but then passing so quickly — became a standard metaphor for the evanescence of life.

One final aside: the imagery of cherries and that of mists, *kasumi*, are often used together in poetry.

古今和歌集　83
　　紀貫之
　　さくらのごととくちる物はなしと人のいひければよめる

桜花　とく散りぬとも　おもほえず　人の心ぞ　風も吹きあへぬ
sakurabana　toku chirinu tomo　omooezu　hito no kokoro zo　kaze mo fukiaenu

　　Kokin Wakashū 83
　　　　Ki no Tsurayuki
　　　　Composed in response to a person commenting that
　　nothing falls quite as fast as cherry blossoms

　　I do not think
　　　　that cherry blossoms scatter
　　　　　　faster than anything
　　Our own hearts
　　　　don't even wait for the wind to blow

千載和歌集　1075
　　源師教朝臣
　　家に櫻をうゑてよみ侍りける

をいが世に　宿にさくらを　移し植ゑて　猶こゝろみに　花を待つかな
oi ga yo ni　yado ni sakura wo　utsushi uete　nao kokoromini　hana wo matsu kana

　　Senzai Wakashū 1075
　　　　Minamoto no Morotaka (Moronori) Ason
　　　　Composed after I planted a cherry in my garden

　　Already settled in my elder years
　　　　I transplanted a cherry tree
　　　　　　to the garden of my house
　　And just to prove the point
　　　　I'm going to wait right here until it blossoms

Shima 島 嶋 Island

The word *shima* means island. Japan is an archipelago made up of four main islands and thousands of smaller ones. The *Chronicles of Japan* describe the very creation of Japan as the act of the male and female gods, Izanagi and Izanami, coupling and giving birth to the eight "big" islands, *ōyashima*: Yamato (Honshū), Tsukushi (Kyūshū), Iyo (Shikoku), which are in fact main islands, and five smaller islands, Awaji, Oki, Tsushima, Iki, and Sado.[161] These were the islands that made up the world-view of the classical-period courtier, along with countless smaller islands and islets. At that time, to travel any distance would likely mean going by boat, and travel by boat meant passing the myriad small islands that pepper the Inland Sea and other coastlines of Japan. In fact, traveling from island to island as a mode of crossing large gaps of water even had a name — *shimazutau*, "going along the islands."[162] Islands, being remote, also served the purpose of being prisons of sorts, and people who were banished from society were at times sent away to distant islands as a means of exile.[163] For these various reasons, the imagery of islands was a familiar and rich one for Heian-period courtiers.

The word *shima*, however, also meant garden in the early classical period. At that time, gardens typically included a pond with an island in it. This was common enough that the word *shima* became a moniker for garden. The Asuka-period (538–710) courtier, Soga no Umako was famous for his garden, which had a pond with an island in it. So impressive was this at that time that he became known as Shima no Ōomi, The Minister of the Island (see previous section on ponds, *ike*).

Islands in gardens are mentioned in many historical records and works of literature. In *Genji Monogatari* we read of cressets being lit on the Middle Isle, *naka-jima*, under a misty moon, and of courtiers boating through a rocky cove in the Middle Isle.[164] But the clearest description of islands in Heian-period gardens comes from the *Sakuteiki* in which there are entire sections devoted to the explanation of how to make an island in a garden pond. To begin with, there were many predetermined styles of islands, including the Mountain Isle, Meadow Isle, Forest Isle, Rocky Shore Isle, Cloud Type, Mist Type, Pebble Beach Type, Slender Stream, Tide Land, and Pine Bark. Each one had a particular feature that distinguished it from the others.[165] The text goes on to give specific design suggestions such as the following:

> Regarding the placement of islands in the pond, first determine the overall size of the pond according to the conditions of the site. As a rule, if conditions will allow it, the side of the central island should be on axis with the center of the main residence. On the back side of this island, a place for musicians should be prepared, as large as twenty-one to twenty-four meters [c. 70 to 80 feet] across. The front of the island should remain plainly visible in front of the musicians' area and so, if there is not enough room on the central island, another island may be constructed behind it and a plank deck constructed to connect the two.[166]

In Poetry

In poetry the word *shima* appears in two ways: first, with the meaning of island and, second, at times in older poems such as those in the *Man'yōshū*, it also was used to mean garden. The poems looked at herein only have to do with *shima* in its meaning of island. There are no specific *makura-kotoba* relationships with the word *shima*. Rather, the poems that include *shima* often simply evoke the scenic quality of islands, sometimes famous islands that are called by name: Awajishima, Mishima, and so on; and more often unknown islands that are simply called *shima*, or *kojima* (small island, islet), or the like. In poems, people look out at them from land, row around them while fishing, pass from one to the next while traveling, and watch cranes fly over them. This last image, of cranes and islands, has an old history. The mystical island Hōrai, that in ancient Chinese legends was described as being the abode of immortals, rested on the backs of huge tortoises. The immortals flew from place to place on the backs of cranes, thus the age-old connection between cranes, tortoises, islands, and the imagery of longevity.

古今和歌集　409
　　このうたは、ある人のいはく、柿本人麿が哥也

ほのぼのと　あかしの浦の　朝霧に　島隠れゆく　舟をしぞ思ふ
honobono to　akashi no ura no　asagiri ni　shimagakure yuku　fune wo shizo omou

　　Kokin Wakashū 409
　　　　According to someone, this poem was composed by
　Kakimoto no Hitomaro

　　　　Seen faintly, only faintly
　　through morning mists that cling
　　　　　　　　to the waters of dawning Akashi Bay
　　　My heart follows a boat
　　　　　　as it slips into the island's shadow

山家集　1356
　　西行
　　同じ國に大師のおはしましける御辺りの山に庵結びて住みけるに月
いと明かくて海の方曇りなく見え侍りければ

曇りなき　山にて海の　月見れば　島ぞこほりの　絶え間なりける
kumori naki　yama nite umi no　tsuki mireba　shima zo kōri no　taema narikeru

　　Sankashū 1356
　　　　Saigyō
　　　　In those same lands (Sanuki), in the mountains where the
　saint priest Kōbō once lived, living in a simple hut, I looked out
　over the bright, moonlit sea on a cloudless night

　　Not a cloud in sight
　　　　looking down from the mountain
　　　　　　　across a sea of moonlight
　　The islands like holes
　　　　in endless sheets of ice

Shimo 霜 Frost

The Element

Shimo means frost, that light covering of crystal ice that whitens the surface of everything on cold mornings. In the central region of Japan, around the capital of Heian, frost was seen from the late autumn through winter. In fact, the 11th month of the Heian-period calendar (or what would equate to around December these days) was known as Shimotsuki, the Frost Month.

In Gardens

Frost, of course, was not introduced into gardens by a designer, the way plants or rocks were, but when it appeared in gardens, it was appreciated by the people who saw it as if it were part of the garden. Deeply so. There are several passages in both *Genji Monogatari* and *Makura no Sōshi* in which the authors praise the beauty of frost. Sometimes this takes place in a natural setting, but often it is in a garden. In the Wakamurasaki chapter of *Genji Monogatari*, for instance, the young girl, Murasaki, newly brought to Genji's Nijō residence, peeks out through the blinds at the autumn garden and finds it "covered with frost and pretty as a picture."[167] Likewise, for Sei Shōnagon, the beauty of frost seems of great enough importance to mention it in the first few lines of her *Makura no Sōshi*.[168]

In Poetry

Frost forms when the weather is cold and although there are some poems that mention frost as a late-winter/early-spring image, most poems use the image of frost to evoke the feeling of late-autumn or early-winter, so much so that *shimo* has become a seasonal marker for that time of year. Also, most poems that use the image of frost are set in the early morning. Thus the stereotypic use of frost in a poem would be one with a scene set at dawn in late autumn.

There are two main aspects of frost that appealed to the people of the

184

Heian period. The first is its whiteness. In the very first passage of *Makura no Sōshi*, as mentioned above, Sei Shōnagon comments on how in winter it is the early mornings that are most beautiful and how splendid they are when everything is white with frost, *shimo no ito shiroki mo*. The second is the effect that frost has on plants, causing them to wilt and bend over. One cold night and life passes, an image that made frost a symbol of the evanescence of life. From the time of the *Man'yōshū*, this was expressed with the phrase *shimo-kare*, or frost-withered. It is also deeply linked to the concept of *utsuroi*, meaning to change or pass into another state. The interesting thing about the sensibility of Heian-period courtiers is that their impression of this change — essentially passing from life to death — was not one of horror or disgust, but one of impassioned pathos and even aesthetic appreciation. The garden is considered all the more beautiful *because* it is in a frost-withered state, passing out of life and into death, the colors of the flowers never more beautiful than that moment when the touch of frost signals their demise.

There are two verbs associated with *shimo*. The first is *oku*, which literally means "to place or put" but could be said here to mean to "settle on," and the second is *furu*, "to fall or precipitate," like falling rain. Of the two, *oku* seems to be the more common, frost having been perceived less as something "falling down" on the earth and more as a phenomenon that is simply "on things."

The last comment about *shimo* is its poetic connection to waterfowl. Many poems capture images of frost-withered inlets, the reeds along the water's edge browning and curling, and waterfowl huddled against the cold. If the birds are *oshi*, Mandarin ducks — which were believed to mate for life and were thus a symbol of fidelity — then the frost on their feathers was an image of the cold world that they protected each other from, at times lightly brushing the frost from each other's wings. One such poem can be found in the previous section on *katsumi*.

千載和歌集　397
　　大炊御門右大臣
　　百首の歌奉りける時初冬の歌によみ侍りける

はつしもや　おきはじむらむ　あか月の　鐘のをとこそ　ほの聞こゆなれ
hatsushimo ya   oki hajimuramu   akatsuki no   kane no oto koso   hono kikoyunare

> *Senzai Wakashū* 397
> Minister of the Right of the Ōimikado
> Composed on the theme of the beginning of winter, for a
presentation of 100 poems

> Could it be this first frost
> 　　settling gently over the land
> In dawn's clear light
> 　　I hear ever so faintly
> 　　　　the sound of a temple bell[169]

後拾遺和歌集　729
　　藤原惟規

霜枯の　かやがしたをれ　とにかくに　思ひ乱れて　過ぐるころかな
shimogare no   kaya ga shita ore   tonikakuni   omoi midarete   suguru koro kana

> *Goshūi Wakashū* 729
> Fujiwara no Nobunori

> Days go by
> 　　all thoughts in confusion
> Cast this way and that
> 　　like the nodded heads
> 　　　　of frost-withered grasses

Shinobu しのぶ Fern

The Element

Shinobu, or *shinobugusa*, is the old name of an evergreen fern, Lepisorus thunbergianus, found throughout Japan, the Korean peninsula, China, and the Himalayas. From ancient times until the Heian period the name was pronounced *shinofu*. Typically it is found growing off of rocks or trees, and is known in Japan for growing on roofs. The leaves of this fern are long and slim, and marked by a pattern of circular dots resulting from the regular rows of sporangium on the back side of the leaves. They usually form clumps or tufts that hang down from whatever they are attached to. Nowadays, *shinobu* is referred to as *noki-shinobu* (roof-eave fern) or, alternatively, *yatsume-ran* (many-eyed orchid).[170]

There is another fern called *shinobu*, Davallia mariesii, that was known from the Nara period. This fern became linked with a form of cloth dying called *shinobu moji zuri*, but it is not the fern that appears in the poems of the day.

In Gardens

There is no evidence that *shinobu* was planted intentionally in gardens in the Heian period, but it is mentioned in literature as growing on the eaves of residences, so it certainly was a part of the garden scene. In the Hashihime chapter of *Genji Monogatari*, the scene is set at the Uji residence of Prince Hachi no Miya, eighth prince of Emperor Kiritsubo, who has renounced the world and devotes himself to raising his daughters. His house and garden, reflective of his state of affairs, are depicted as being in disarray, the garden thick with weeds and *shinobu* growing on the eaves of the house.[171] In the Yūgao and Yomogiu chapters we find similar scenes in which *shinobu* growing on the eaves of a residence or gate is a sign that the household in question has fallen on hard times.[172]

Sei Shōnagon, in *Makura no Sōshi*, describes *shinobu* as being incredibly vigorous in its ability to grow and spread and says she thinks the plant makes such a beautiful picture, hanging off the edge of things.[173]

In Poetry

There are two words also pronounced *shinobu*, that give a deep symbolic meaning to the use of this fern in literature. The first, written 忍ぶ, means to conceal oneself, to hide or to endure. This meaning was used in older literature but, by the time of the Heian period, had given way to the second word, written 偲ぶ, that means to recollect or to remember. Although the word *shinobu* was typically written phonetically, thus not stipulating which meaning was intended, the situation of the passages made clear that the image of reflection — in particular reflection on events of the past — was intended. Such was the case for introducing *shinobu* into the scene mentioned above at the residence of Hachi no Miya who spends his time in lonely sadness reflecting on his wife who passed away giving birth to his second daughter.

Shinobu-gusa is also linked, as an *engo*, to the word *shigeru*, which means to grow thickly or to be luxuriously verdant. This usage in poems brings to mind not only thick bunches of *shinobu-gusa* growing, usually off the eaves of a roof, but also the richness and complexity of the feelings the author of the poem is experiencing as he or she wanders through past memories.

千載和歌集　856
　　前参議親隆

東屋の　を萱の軒の　しのぶ草　しのびもあへず　茂る思ひに
azumaya no　ogaya no noki no　shinobugusa　shinobi mo aezu　shigeru omoi ni

> *Senzai Wakashū* 856
>
> > Former Councilor Chikataka
>
> Like the ferns
> > that cluster on the eaves
> > > of this thatch-roofed hut
> My imagination runs rampant
> > with thoughts I cannot bear

古今和歌集　200
　　読人知らず

君しのぶ　草にやつるる　故里は　まつ虫の音ぞ　かなしかりける
kimi shinobu　kusa ni yatsururu　furusato wa　matsumushi no ne zo　kanashikarikeru

> *Kokin Wakashū* 200
>
> > Anonymous
>
> Biding my time in this battered home
> > dotted with ferns of memory
> > > lost in thoughts of you
> Pine cricket cries fill the air
> > with sadness

Susuki 薄 Silver Grass

The Element

Susuki, Miscanthus sinensis, is a tall perennial grass, often reaching 2 meters (6.5 feet) in height, that grows over large areas in meadows as well as along banks of rivers and ponds. It has at least three names in Japanese: *susuki* 薄, as already mentioned, as well as *obana* 尾花 and *kaya* 萱. The usage of these different terms is not fixed, but *susuki* is more often used as a general term; *obana* has a somewhat more poetic feeling; and *kaya* is the word typically used for the grass when it is used as thatch, thus the term *kayabuki yane,* or thatched-roof house. If fact, *kaya* can refer to any grass used for thatching or that is useful in village life such as *ogi* (Miscanthus sacchariflorus, Amur silver-grass), *chigaya* (Imperata cylindrica var. koenigii, Japanese blood grass), and *suge* (various plants in the genus Carex, sedges). In English, *susuki* has several names including miscanthus, silver grass, maidenhair grass, and eulalia.

Susuki would have been a common sight for the Heian-period courtiers, since many meadows still existed around the capital and the grass was used in various aspects of rural life, especially the aforementioned roof thatching. The word *karu* means to cut or harvest, thus *karu kaya* would translate as harvest-grass or harvested-grass. *Susuki* that has been cut is referred to as *karu kaya*, but there is also another plant, Themeda japonica (T. triandra var. japonica), unrelated to *susuki*, which is called *karu kaya*.

Perhaps the most distinctive aspect of *susuki* is the flower/seed heads (inflorescence) that the plant produces in autumn. These puffy, white clusters sit high above the already tall leaves, swaying gracefully in any breeze. In many ways they look like bushy tails, thus the name *obana,* which means "tail-flower." Because of this spectacular show in autumn, the image of *susuki* became inherently linked to that season.

In Gardens

In the Fuji no Uraba chapter of *Genji Monogatari*, *susuki* is described in the Sanjō palace. The palace is run down and clumps of *susuki* have become overgrown. The word used to describe this state is *midare*, the "state of confusion" that is often linked with *susuki* in poetry.[174] In the Kashiwagi chapter, again the garden has a clump of *susuki*, this time laden with dew and filled with crying crickets, all being signs of autumn.[175]

Genji Monogatari Emaki, an illustrated scroll created within 100 years of the writing of *Genji Monogatari*, is the closest thing we have to visual documentation of court life during the Heian period. The condition of the scrolls is not perfect, and only a few of the many original scrolls are extant. Most of the scenes are interiors but some depict parts of the story that take place on or near the veranda, and the garden is shown in the background or foreground — albeit not clearly. In several of these scenes, tall arching grasses can be seen that would appear to be *susuki*.

In Poetry

As mentioned, *susuki* is thought of as an autumn plant and one linked to the image of meadows, *no* in Japanese, so *susuki* shows up in poetry in connection to famous meadows such as Yamatoji and Urano.[176] When expressed as *obana*, which literally means "tail-flower," a poetic link is often made to the word *ho*, the inflorescence of the grass, which is the plume-like tassel of flowers/seeds that grows over the blades of grass in autumn.

Karu kaya, harvested grass, takes on some new meanings when it is used as a pillow word. When *kaya* is cut for use, it is typically tied up into manageable bundles before being carried off. Thus the image of cut *kaya* links to the word bundle, *tsuka*, and from there to the expression *tsuka no ma*, meaning a brief moment of time or transient. If one doesn't bundle *kaya* when it is cut, it immediate falls this way and that making a scene of great confusion, an image that forms the basis for a second pillow word connection. In this case *kaya* is used to link to the word *midaru*, to be confused, and *omoi-midaru* or to have confused thoughts/memories, as presented in the discussion of *makura-kotoba* in the Heian-period Poetry section above.

古今和歌集　653
　　　小野春風

花すすき　穂にいでて恋ひば　名を惜しみ　下結ふ紐の　むすぼほれつつ
hana susuki　ho ni idete koiba　na wo oshimi　shita yū himo no　musuboore tsutsu

Kokin Wakashū 653

　　Ono no Harukaze

If I was to love you　　as openly
　　as the plumes of autumn meadow grass
　　　　I fear whispers would disgrace my name
So tighten the braids of my under garments
　　and twist my heart into knots

万葉集　3065

み吉野の　秋津の小野に　刈る草の　思ひ乱れて　寝る夜しぞ多き
miyoshino no　akizu no ono ni　karu kaya no　omoimidarete　nuru yo shizo ōki

Man'yōshū 3065

In beautiful Yoshino
　　the dragonfly fields of Akizu
　　　　are strewn with cut grasses
My thoughts scatter as wildly
　　troubling many an evening's sleep

Take 竹 Bamboo

There were several varieties of bamboo that were variously referred to as *take*, *shino*, and *sasa* and variants thereof.[177] There are many possibilities of which bamboos these names referred to. *Take* may have referred to one of the large bamboos, the most likely possibility being *madake* (Phyllostachys bambusoides, 真竹). The other large-scale bamboo commonly found in Japan today, *mōsōchiku* (Phyllostachys edulis or P. pubescens or P. heterocycla, 孟宗竹), was imported to Japan from China during a later era. Another expression commonly found for bamboo is *kuretake* (also pronounced *gochiku*, 呉竹). *Kure* was the name that the Japanese used to refer to China in ancient times so the name *kuretake* implies that this was, originally, an imported plant. *Kuretake* was most likely the plant that is now called *hachiku* (Phyllostachys nigra var. henonis, 淡竹), a medium-scale bamboo that is the likely parent of the now popular black bamboo, *kurotake* (黒竹). *Shino*, written variously 篠, 小竹, and 細竹, probably referred to the smaller caliper bamboos such as *medake* (Pleioblastus simonii, 女竹) or *yadake* (Pseudosasa japonica, 矢竹), the latter of which was used to make arrows. And, finally, there are references to *sasa*, the smaller, more delicate-stemmed grass bamboos such as those in the Sasa genus like *kumazasa* (Sasa veitchii, 隈笹).

All bamboos are grasses, the stems of which can be .3 cm (1/8 inch) thick, in the case of *sasa*, or 13 cm to 16 cm (five to six inches) thick, in the case of *madake*. The heights also range greatly, from 30 cm to 60 cm (one to two feet) for low-growing *sasa*, to up to 18 meters (60 feet) for the tallest *madake*. Once the roots are established, the full height of the plant is achieved in one growing season — at times within a few weeks. It is for this reason that bamboo has become linked to the image of vitality and energetic growth.

In Gardens

Large-scale bamboo may have been planted in gardens but it is unlikely that any except the largest garden would have been able to accommodate these vigorously growing plants. It was, however, definitely used in gardens of all sizes to make things like fences and water pipes. In the Hashihime chapter of *Genji Monogatari*, for instance, we find a mention of a bamboo lattice fence. Bamboo lattice fences (*suigai* or *sukashigaki*) are either made of slats of bamboo split from a large-scale culm like that of *madake* and then woven into an open lattice, or they can be made of stems of a smaller-scale bamboo bound together in an open framework.[178] The water pipes were certainly made of a large-scale bamboo — the smaller types being too narrow to work effectively. To make a water pipe, the bamboo is cut into lengths and then the solid nodes inside of the stem are punched out with a long stick to create a long, hollow tube. These could then be used — above ground or underground — to channel water through the garden. The following quote is from the *Sakuteiki*.

> If a man-made wellspring is to be used to feed a well, then construct a large water tank on a high pedestal next to the well. Beneath this build a box pipe as mentioned before, and connect the bottom of the tank to the top of the box-pipe with a bamboo pipe, thereby feeding water from the tank into the pipe. Water will be caused to gush out from the well; a vision of coolness.[179]

Another way in which bamboo was used was during the construction of a garden was as a level-measuring device. When laying out a stream it was important to understand how much slope was available across a garden. Likewise, when digging out a pond, one needed to understand which points along the shoreline were at the same level. In order to determine this, a long piece of thick bamboo would be split in half, making a long thin trough. Filled with water, this trough could be used to determine level points, or measured off of to determine slope. The *Sakuteiki* states it this way.

> Since the slope of the stream is difficult to perceive while it is under construction, place a length of bamboo that has been split in half lengthways on the ground and fill it with water in order to determine the slope of the ground.[180]

The *Sakuteiki* does not mention bamboo being planted in the garden but it does mention *sasa*. It suggests, to create the Reed Style of garden, *ashide no yō*, that stones should be placed along meadows or at the water's edge and, next to them, grass-like plants like *sasa* should be planted.[181]

In *Genji Monogatari* we find many mentions of *kuretake* being grown in the garden, especially in that part of the garden close to the residence known as the *senzai*, near garden. One such scene was mentioned in the introduction in which Prince Genji is pursuing a young girl, Tamakazura. He sees in the garden a patch of Chinese bamboo, *kuretake*, and is pleased by the flexibility of the young plant.[182] Sei Shōnagon, in her *Makura no Sōshi,* mentions bamboo growing near the Seiryō Palace, and also includes bamboo in her description of Outstandingly Splendid Things, *yo ni medetaki mono*, in which elegant dancers wind their way through a grove of bamboo.[183]

Seasonally, bamboo is usually considered an indicator of winter. This is because it is evergreen, and because of the lovely curved shapes it attains when weighted down with snow. And yet, only a few poems actually describe bamboo in winter.

In literature — such as the *Kojiki*, *Genji Monogatari*, and *Taketori Monogatari* — there are passages that describe the incredible vigor or magical life-force of bamboo. This imagery is, however, only at times apparent in poetry. Rather, most poems that use bamboo symbolically do so in one of two ways. The most common way relates to the fact that bamboo grows in a series of distinct sections — empty tubes separated by solid diaphragms called nodes. In Japanese the node is called a *fushi* 節. The length between the nodes is called a *yo*, which is written, oddly enough, with the same character as *fushi*. The word *yo*, however, can be written with other characters. Written 世 it means "the world" or "society," and written 代 it means "generations." As such, bamboo is used in poems that relate to human relations in the world, the passage of time, or a wish for long life. Secondly, because the imperial court was referred to as the Bamboo Grove, *take no sono'u* (竹の園生), bamboo in poetry (especially the expression *sasu take no*) came to be linked to expressions such as *kimi* (lord), *miko* (child of the emperor or shrine maiden), and *miyabito* (courtier).

古今和歌集　957
　　よみ人知らず
　　物思ひける時、いときなきこを見てよめる

いまさらに　なに生ひいづらむ　竹の子の　優き節しげき　よとは知らずや
imasara ni　nani oiizuramu　take no ko no　uki fushi shigeki　yo to wa shirazu ya

　　Kokin Wakashū 957
　　　　Anonymous
　　　　Composed upon seeing an innocent child at a time when
　　I was filled with worry

　　　　At such a time as this
　　　　　　why were you born at all
　　　　Rising into a world as filled with grief
　　　　　　as the countless nodes
　　　　　　　　on a bamboo shoot

万葉集　955
　　大宰少弐石川朝臣足人歌一首

さす竹の　大宮人の　家と住む　佐保の山をば　思ふやも君
sasu take no　ōmiyahito no　ie to sumu　saho no yama woba　omou yamo kimi

　　Man'yōshū 955
　　　　Junior Assistant Governor-General (Dazai no Shōni),
　　Ishikawa no Asomi Taruhito

　　　　And you
　　　　　　don't you think fondly
　　　　　　　　on the hills of Saoyama
　　　　Where our courtiers make their homes
　　　　　　and thrive like spreading bamboo

Taki 滝 瀧 Waterfall

The word *taki* has two related meanings. The most common meaning, certainly in modern Japanese, is that of water dropping from a high place, in other words a waterfall. In modern Japanese this is written 滝 but the old character, which is still used, is 瀧. The second meaning, which as you will see is closely related but was more common in classical periods than now, is that of a place in a stream where the water moves forward with great energy — seething and boiling. Through the Nara period, *tagi* was the pronunciation, changing to *taki* during the Heian period.

The native religion of Japan is now called Shintō, the Way of the Gods. Although the use of this unifying name doesn't begin until after the Heian period, many of the various religious practices that make up Shintō were established long before that era. One of these was the worshiping of *kami*, god-spirits, in natural settings — forests, mountains, seasides, etc. — through the medium of certain distinctive natural elements, such as oddly-shaped or prominent boulders, huge ancient trees, and waterfalls. Among these waterfalls, perhaps the most famous is the 130-meter (426 feet) Nachi no Taki at the Hirō Shrine in the Kumano district of Wakayama Prefecture, but there are many many others that are smaller at shrines throughout Japan.[184] Buddhist temples were also sited near waterfalls, and the Buddhist deity, Fudō Myōō, is in particular seen as being associated with waterfalls.[185] Sculptures of Fudō are often found near waterfalls and practitioners of ascetic Buddhism will stand with the waterfall cascading down on their head and shoulders while they pray to Fudō.

In Gardens

We know for certain that the design of gardens included the use of

198

waterfalls during the Heian period. Prince Genji is described making a waterfall in the garden of Akikonomu at the Rokujō palace, but by far our clearest descriptions of waterfalls in Heian-period gardens comes from the *Sakuteiki*. The *Sakuteiki* has an entire section devoted to nothing but the design and construction of waterfalls.[186] Included are technical advice for construction, points on aesthetic design, as well as the Buddhist meaning of waterfalls. An example of each follows:

> … first set a Waterfall Stone with a good surface, one that seems as if it will harmonize with the Bracketing Stones. Then pack soil in and around the base of the stone so that it will not budge so much as a speck, and finally reinforce it with well-fitted Bracketing Stones. After all this, pack all the gaps between the stones with clay and then again with a mixture of soil and gravel. One should strictly adhere to these steps when making a waterfall.

> … waterfalls appear graceful when they flow out unexpectedly from narrow crevices between stones half-hidden in shadows. At the source of the waterfall, just above the Waterfall Stone, some well-chosen stones should be placed so that, when seen from afar, the water will appear to be flowing out from the crevices of those boulders, creating a splendid effect.

> Fudō Myōō has vowed that "all waterfalls over 90 centimeters in height are expressions of my self." …. All waterfalls are surely expressions of a Buddhist Trinity: the two flanking stones, to the right and left of the dominant

stone, probably represent the Buddha's attendants.

There were many kinds of waterfalls in Heian-period gardens according to the *Sakuteiki*, including a double-streamed Twin Fall (*mukai-ochi*, 向い 落), a Leaping Fall (*hanare-ochi*, 離れ落) from which water jumps outward, the Cloth Fall (*nuno-ochi*, 布落) in which the water flows smoothly across a rock face like a cloth, and the Thread Fall (*ito-ochi*, 糸落) where the water crosses a saw-toothed edge and breaks into thin thread-like white streams.

In Poetry

In poetry, *taki* shows up in both of the two meanings mentioned above. *Taki no ito*, "waterfall threads," is a poetic expression that describes the image of the Thread Fall mentioned above in which a waterfall breaks into thin streams. But typically the image of the waterfall in poems — whether a falling waterfall or a rushing stream — is that of relentless energy or urgency, expressive of uncontrollable amorous emotions.

Taki, as both the "falling waterfall" and the "rushing stream," shows up in poetry in several forms with diverse symbolic purposes. *Taki no mizu*, the water of the waterfall, links to the word *sumu* which means "clear" as in crystal clear water, but it also further links to another word pronounced *sumu*, that means to "live somewhere." *Taki* can also link to the word *oto*, meaning sound, and thus further link to the word *uwasa*, or rumors. But the most common symbolic meaning related to *taki* in poetry is that of incessant energy or urgency, signalling uncontrollable feelings of love. The term most often used in this regard is *takitsu*, or *tagitsu*, as in the *makura-kotoba*, *takitsu-se-no*, of the rushing torrent.

And then, of course, there's the waterfall of tears, *namida no taki*.

古今和歌集　491

あしひきの　山下水の　木隠くれて　たぎつ心を　堰きぞかねつる

ashihiki no   yama shita mizu no   kogakurete   tagitsu kokoro wo   seki zo kanetsuru

Kokin Wakashū 491

The waters of the torrent
    at the base of the mountain
        run hidden through deep trees
Hold as I might   the secrets of my heart
    they cascade beyond control

山家集　　1118
　　西行
　　三重の瀧を拝みけるに、殊にたふとく覺えて三業の罪もすゝがるゝ
心地してければ

身に積る　言葉の罪も　洗はれて　心澄みぬる　三重の滝

mi ni tsumoru   kotoba no tsumi mo   arawarete   kokoro suminuru   mikasane no taki

Sankashū 1118
    Saigyō
    While worshipping at three-tiered Mie Waterfall, I found
    it especially precious, and felt as if cleansed of the Sins of the
    Three Actions [Deeds, Words, and Thoughts]

Washed clean
    of even the sins of speech
        layered on my earthly self
My spirit serene   made pure
    by the three-tiered falls

TAKE

imasara ni
nani oiizuramu
take no ko no
uki fushi shigeki
yo to wa shirazu ya
Kokin Wakashū 957

BAMBOO

At such a time as this
why were you born at all
Rising into a world as filled with grief
as the countless nodes
on a bamboo shoot

Tsuki 月 Moon

The Element

The word *tsuki* means moon. The moon, of course, needs no introduction except to stress the importance it plays in Japanese culture. Moon-viewing was, and still is, an important seasonal ritual. In the Heian period, festivals to watch the moon, *tsukimi*, were held on the evenings of the 15th day of the 8th month and the 13th day of the 9th month of the old lunar calendar. Records of the lives of Heian-period courtiers, such as *Genji Monogatari* and *Makura no Sōshi*, reveal that a great deal of social interaction happened at night. This was not limited only to men prowling about to find their lovers (although that is often the case) but also includes many scenes when the entire household of a particular residence is up in the evening, enjoying some pastime or other in the garden, either by the light of burning cressets or simply by the moonlight alone.

People thought of the moon in two opposing ways. First, as being the embodiment of evil or as something taboo, and second as a thing that was beautiful and mysterious. The first perception, that the moon was taboo, was somewhat stronger in pre-Heian times, changing during the Heian period to a focus on the moon's beauty. But the change was not complete. An early Heian-period folktale, *Taketori Monogatari* (*The Tale of the Bamboo Cutter*), that centers on a celestial princess who visits the earth from the moon, contains a line in its ending passages that warns that it is taboo to look on the face of the moon. That doing so will only bring sadness.[187] In *Genji Monogatari*, although references to the moon are overwhelmingly positive, some of the old perception of the moon as taboo can still be sensed. In the Yadorigi chapter, there is a passage in which the moon is repeatedly woven into the scene between Niou and Nakanokimi to reflect their troubled emotions. Nakanokimi, gazing on the moon, is advised not to do so because looking on the moon is taboo.[188]

In Gardens

In gardens from the 17th century onward, we find the construction of a deck called a *tsukimi-dai*, moon-viewing platform. It is very clear from the name alone that the purpose of the platform was to provide a place from which to watch the moon. When situated near a body of water, the reflection of the rising moon could be viewed as well. There is no specific term *tsukimi-dai* in Heian-period texts, but people are often noted gazing at the moon either from the garden itself, or from a nearby building or, more likely, from the veranda of that building.

In Poetry

In poems the moon may be expressed as *tsuki* or *tsukikage*. *Kage* is an interesting word, referring to a light or a darkness, or anything projected. Shadows were seen not as the absence of light, but as a darkness projected from objects. And, *tsuki-kage* which literally means "the moon projected," is moonlight.

Even though, as can be told by the dates of the festivals mentioned above, the favored season for moon viewing is autumn, in *Genji Monogatari* we find scenes in which people are enjoying moonlight in almost every season. There is even a scene in which there is a debate between which is more beautiful: moonlight in spring or in autumn.[189] So the moon is not really a poetic symbol of any particular season.

Melancholy and beauty, and at times spiritual enlightenment, are what come to mind most in relation to the moon and how it is expressed in poems and literature. Moonlight falling on spring flowers, or over the autumn mountains, or on a frozen lake. It is at once eerily mysterious, emotive, tinged with sadness, and also extremely beautiful.

後撰和歌集　336

秋風に　いとゞふけゆく　月影を　立ちな隠しそ　天の川霧
akikaze ni　itodo fukeyuku　tsukikage wo　tachi na kakushi so　ama no kawagiri

Gosen Wakashū 336

Autumn breezes blow
    as moonlight grows brighter and brighter
        by the hour
Mists along Heaven's River
    please don't conceal this

❧   ❦

山家集　522
    西行
    庭上冬月といふ事を

さゆと見えて　冬深くなる　月影は　水なき庭に　氷をぞしく
sayu to miete　fuyu fukaku naru　tsukikage wa　mizu naki niwa ni　kōri wo zo shiku

Sankashū 522

    Saigyō
    Composed about the moon hanging above a winter garden

Winter deepens
    the moonlight appears so intensely
        cold and serene
Spreading out like ice slicks
    across the waterless garden

Tsuyu 露 Dew

The Element

Tsuyu means dew, the fine droplets of water that cling to surfaces of things outside on cool mornings. The generally high moisture levels in Japan and cool autumn weather combine to allow for the easy formation of dew in the mornings in that season.

In Gardens

That dew existed in gardens in the Heian period goes without saying — if it settles anywhere in Japan it would also settle in the gardens — but it is revealing of a cultural trait that dew in gardens should be mentioned so often in the literature of the time. In *Genji Monogatari*, time and time again, the flowers and grasses of the garden are noted as being thick with dew or covered with drops of dew sparking like jewels. As we will see below, this interest goes beyond the simple sparkly beauty of the scene because, for Heian-period courtiers, dew was imbued with certain poetic meanings.

There are some scenes in which the mention of dew sheds light on certain aspects of court life such as the one in the Nowaki chapter of *Genji Monogatari* in which Akikonomu, the Empress who lived by the autumn-themed garden, sends her page girls among the garden plants to collect dew to feed to their caged crickets.[190] Sei Shōnagon, in *Makura no Sōshi* comments on how beautiful things look with dew on them. She points out, at different times in the book, dew on chrysanthemums (*kiku*, with floss silk on them to absorb the dew and scent[191]), bush clover (*hagi*, dew on a sprig attached to a letter), cherry blossoms (*sakura*, blossoms wet with dew are magnificent), bloodgrass (*asaji*, glittering like jewels), a spider's web (*kumo no su*, like strings of white pearls), and garden grasses (*omae no kusa*, leave them tall so that they show off the dew).[192]

In Poetry

Although there are some spring and summer poems that use dew as an image — dew on the summer-flowering lotus, for instance, is not uncommon — the season most readily associated with dew is autumn. Cold, bleak, and sad. Dew is often connected, poetically, to a particular place or time, so we find *asatsuyu*, morning dew; *yūtsuyu*, evening dew; *uwatsuyu*, upper dew (dew on the tops of leaves of plants); and *shitatsuyu*, lower dew (dew on the forest floor). And dew is associated with certain verbs: *koboru*, to spill; *kakaru*, to hang upon; *kiyu*, to disappear; and so on.

Shiny and round, drops of dew are often likened to jewels. A favorite expression, *shiratsuyu*, or white-dew, brings to mind the image of pearls but the exact type of jewel is never stated, only the word *tama* which can mean a drop (of rain, dew, or tears), a sphere, or a jewel when written one way, 玉, or the soul when written another, 魂, thus connecting the word to a broad range of poetic meanings.

Although *tsuyu* can be used in poems simply to indicate the season or to comment on the beauty of nature, there are two overriding symbolic usages: dew as a symbol for tears, and as a symbol of evanescence. When poets describe a scene in which the weight of gathered dew has bent the supple branches of the bush clover, they are usually depicting an atmosphere of sadness, the dew standing in for tears, *namida*, the weighted down branches equated to the disconsolate mood of the poets themselves.

Because dew typically evaporates a few hours after dawn, it became an apt symbol of things that are transient, *hakanashi*, life and love being the two favorite subjects. Dew on flowers — both being symbols of evanescence — heightens the expression of the poet even further, so we find references to dew on cherries, chrysanthemums, lotuses, bush clovers, and, the favorite ephemeral pair, dew on *asagao*.[193] Along with flower blossoms, spider webs are delicate things that last only for a short time, so we find drops of dew on spider webs as another image of transience. In line with this, poems might describe how the wind will come and tear the dew off the plants it was clinging to, the images of confusion, *midareru*, and evanescence blending to evoke the pathos of the author.

古今和歌集　860
　　藤原惟幹
　　身まかりなむとてよめる

露をなど　あだなるものと　思ひけむ　わが身も草に　置かぬばかりを
tsuyu wo nado　adanaru mono to　omoikemu　wagami mo kusa ni　okanu bakari wo

　　　　Kokin Wakashū 860
　　　　　　Fujiwara no Koremoto
　　　　　　Composed on the brink of death

　　Why did I think
　　　　the evanescent thing
　　　　　　was just the dew
　　When I too am but a breath
　　　　from lying with the grass

万葉集　1617
　　山口女王<贈>大伴宿祢家持歌一首

秋萩に　置きたる露の　風吹きて　落つる涙は　留めかねつも
aki hagi ni　okitaru tsuyu no　kaze fukite　otsuru namida wa　todome kanetsu mo

　　　　Man'yōshū 1617
　　　　　　The imperial princess, Yamaguchi no Nyoō presented this
　　poem to Ōtomo no Yakamochi

　　Like dew that rested on
　　　　the autumn bush clover
　　　　　　blown free by the winds
　　My falling teardrops
　　　　showed no sign of stopping

Uguisu 鶯 Bush Warbler

The Element

The *uguisu*, Cettia diphone, is a small song bird, about the size of a sparrow. It is usually called the Japanese bush warbler and at times the Japanese nightingale although it does not, in fact, sing in the evening, something noted by Sei Shōnagon in her *Makura no Sōshi* as one of her few complaints about the otherwise praiseworthy bird. The *uguisu* is not a conspicuous bird — its color is a demure green-brown, and its habits are secretive, tending to remain hidden in the shadows of trees and thickets. Although omnivorous, its predilection is for insects, which make up the bulk of its diet. Sei Shōnagon mentions that another name for the bird is "insect-eater," *mushi-kui*. What is outstanding about this little bird is its song, which begins in late spring and continues through the summer to autumn.[194] Especially because the bird itself is so hard to see, the sharp, clear, flute-like trilling often seems to simply come out of thin air.

In Gardens

Uguisu were regular visitors in spring to the garden according to many Heian-period accounts. In the Maboroshi chapter of *Genji Monogatari* we find Genji sitting in front of his garden in the 2nd month and, though most of the garden is veiled in mist, he can see a red plum in flower — planted it would seem in the *senzai*, the "front garden," and thus within view from the residence — and notices a warbler that alights in it. This brings to mind his recently deceased love, Murasaki no Ue for whom this garden was created, and he composes a poem, waxing sentimental on warblers, plums, and the evanescence of life.[195]

Sei Shōnagon, in the same section of *Makura no Sōshi* mentioned above, has quite a bit to say about the *uguisu*. Although she agrees with the poets who praise the bird's virtues, she wonders why it won't sing in the imperial palace, even though it sings loudly in the garden of a commoner. She also claims that, although the song of the *uguisu* is excellent in spring, by summer and into autumn it becomes a hoarse shadow of its former glory, and regrets that it can't simply confine itself to spring when it is at its best.

In Poetry

Uguisu in poetry is one of the quintessential symbols of spring. The image of the bird is often linked with a plant. *Take* (bamboo), *unohana* (deutzia), *yamabuki* (kerria), and *yanagi* (willow) are all possibilities but by far the most common is *ume* (plum). The image of an *uguisu* in a plum tree has become a classic metaphor. The problem is, *uguisu*, being shy creatures that like to stay hidden in woods and thickets seeking the insects they find there, are not likely to be found out in the open, in a garden in a flowering tree like a plum. Then again, another small song bird, the *mejiro*, the Japanese white-eye (Zosterops japonicus) loves the nectar of the plum blossom and is known to visit plums in spring. Certainly most photographs you find these days of a small bird in a plum tree are likely to be of a *mejiro* not an *uguisu*.

万葉集　837
　　算師志氏大道

春の野に　鳴くやうぐひす　なつけむと　我が家の園に　梅が花咲く
haru no no ni　naku ya uguisu　natsukemu to　waga e no sono ni　ume ga hana saku

Man'yōshū 837
　　Sanshishiji no Ōmichi

As if to win the hearts
　　of the warblers　　singing so sweetly
　　　　in the meadow flushed with spring
The plum blossoms opened
　　smiling on my garden

古今和歌集　106
　　読人しらず

吹く風を　なきてうらみよ　鶯は　我やは花に　手だにふれたる
fuku kaze wo　nakite urami yo　uguisu wa　ware ya wa hana ni　te dani furetaru

Kokin Wakashū 106
　　Anonymous

Oh bush warbler
　　blow your sweet curses
　　　　to the wind　　not me
I have not so much as lifted a finger
　　to scatter all these blossoms

Ume 梅 Plum

To begin with, there are some overlapping terms that need to be clarified. The plant that the Japanese call *ume*, which is the focus of this section, is not in fact a plum but is properly called the Japanese apricot (梅, Prunus mume). The plant that produces a fruit we would call a plum is known as *sumomo* in Japan (李, Prunus salicina), and the plant that produces what we call the apricot fruit is called *anzu* (杏, Prunus armeniaca). That said, for poetic and historical reasons, in our translations and text here, we will continue to refer to the *ume* as a plum. Bad habits die hard.

Botanically, the *ume* has its origins in central China and was introduced to Japan in the Nara period (710–784). It shows up with great regularity in the texts from that period onward. The flower of the tree is profuse: white, pale pink, or red, depending on the variety. The fruit of the *ume* can be pickled to make a sour preserved fruit, known as *umeboshi*, that is used as a condiment.

According to the Chinese-style design of Japanese imperial palaces, to the south of the main hall was an open courtyard spread with sand that was used as an entry and a gathering area. At the bottom of the central stairs that led up from the courtyard into the main hall, to the right and left, were planted two trees: one deciduous and one evergreen. The deciduous tree was originally an *ume*, only to be replaced by a cherry in the 9th century.[196]

In Gardens

We know that *ume* were planted in gardens from a variety of sources. The first is archeological digs of Heian-period gardens that have discovered remnants of plums such as the seed pits of the fruits.[197] Sei Shōnagon

213

mentions plums in the imperial garden, with white ones being planted to the west and red ones to the east.[198] Although references are made to both white and red, it is the red plum, *kōbai*, that is much more frequently mentioned. Plums are mentioned very frequently in *Genji Monogatari*, which has two chapters that even have plums in their titles. Often the plum trees are described as being planted in the "near garden," *senzai*, which was the section closest to the residence.[199]

In Poetry

Ume shows up in poetry profusely. In the ancient anthology called the *Man'yōshū*, it is second only to *hagi*, the bush clover, in its number of appearances. In the early years this could have been attributed to the fact that the tree was newly imported from China and thus exotic, but it remained a consistent part of literature long after that initial attraction must have faded, showing how deeply it had been accepted as a part of Japanese culture.

Above all else, in poetry the plum is the classic symbol of spring, *haru*, or the coming of spring because of its early flowering. A bird whose bright song punctuates the world in spring is the bush warbler, *uguisu*. It is not uncommon to find poems that mention all three: *haru*, *uguisu*, and *ume* one right after the other.

The flowers of the plum are profuse and they are subtly fragrant. The *Man'yōshū* doesn't mention scents, but from that time on later poems often link the image of *ume* with its fragrance.

古今和歌集　41
　　凡河内躬恒
　　はるのよ梅花をよめる

春の夜の　闇はあやなし　梅の花　色こそ見えね　香やはかくるる
haru no yo no   yami wa ayanashi   ume no hana   iro koso miene   ka ya wa kakururu

> *Kokin Wakashū* 41
>
> > Ōshikōchi no Mitsune
> >
> > A poem for plum blossoms on a spring night
>
> The darkness isn't
> > very clever this spring night
>
> Covering up the colors
> > of the plum blossom
> >
> > > and forgetting its perfume

万葉集 1854

うぐひすの　木伝ふ梅の　うつろへば　桜の花の　時かたまけぬ
uguisu no   kozutau ume no   utsuroeba   sakura no hana no   toki katamakenu

> *Man'yōshū* 1854
>
> The plum branches
> > where the warbler used to flit
> >
> > > have begun to fade
>
> The time is now ripe
> > for cherry blossoms

Unohana 卯の花 Deutzia

The Element

Unohana is the name used in classical literature for the plant that is now called *utsugi*, Deutzia crenata. In English the plant is known simply as deutzia. In fact in the Heian period, both *unohana* and *utsuki* (the last syllable being *ki* not *gi*) were used. The Japanese name, *utsugi*, has several linguist derivations. Written 卯木 it means, literally, Tree of the Fourth Month, that month being the traditional time for planting rice in the paddies. Written with other characters, 空木, the literal meaning becomes "the hollow tree," which refers to the hollow stem of the shrub. *Unohana* is a shrub of the hydrangea family that grows naturally in mountain meadows to about 2 meters (6.5 feet) in height and has profuse white blossoms in early summer.

In Gardens

In the Otome chapter of *Genji Monogatari,* we find *unohana* mentioned as a hedge, *unohana no kakine*, in the garden at the Rokujō palace. This is the garden that had four separate quadrants for four ladies; and the *unohana* was planted in the garden of Hanachirusato who lived in the northeast section which was the garden designed for summer.[200] In *Makura no Sōshi*, Sei Shōnagon describes the *unohana* as an ordinary flower, unworthy of praise. The white blooms against the green leaves reminds her of summer-weight robes, the white cloth of the undergarments showing against the yellow-green outer robe. She mentions passing hedges of *unohana* on the way to the Kamo Shrine and how her servants pluck sprays of blossoms to decorate her carriage with.[201]

Unohana was a symbol of summer. Despite the fact that its name could potentially refer to the 4th month, *unohana* was linked in poetry to the 5th month, *satsuki*, and to the long rains that come at that time known as *samidare*. The *hototogisu* or cuckoo, being a bird associated with the 5th month, is often found mentioned in combination with the *unohana* flowers.

Another connection in poetry occurs because the "*u*" sound in *unohana* linguistically links to the "*u*" sound in *uki* (憂き) or *uku* (憂く), which mean misery, distress, or hardship. This can be seen, for instance, in the following poem from the *Gosen Wakashū* in which *unohana no* is introduced as a *makura kotoba* that leads to the word *uku*. As such, the use of *unohana* in a poem can lead into either images of summer and summer rains or thoughts of distress and the misery of life.

後撰和歌集　154
　　友達のとぶらひまでこぬ事を恨みつかはすとて

白妙に　にほふかきねの　卯花の　憂くも來てとふ　人のなきかな
shiratae ni　niou kakine no　unohana no　uku mo kite tou　hito no naki kana

> *Gosen Wakashū* 154
>
> Written in reproach of friends who never come to visit

My beautiful garden hedge
　　filled with deutzia blossoms
　　　　brilliant as white cloth
Yet no one stops to see this sight
　　my only visitor — sadness

万葉集　4217
　　霖雨晴日作歌一首

卯の花を　腐す霖雨の　始水に　寄るこつみなす　寄らむ児もがも
unohana wo　kutasu nagame no　hanamizu ni　yoru kotsumi nasu　yoramu ko mo gamo

> *Man'yōshū* 4217
>
> Written during the rainy season on a day when the
> weather cleared

The flood waters
　　from endless showers
　　　　ruin the white flowers
Bring bits of flotsam and jetsam
　　why not a girl for me

Yama 山 Mountain

The Element

The word *yama* means mountain and Japan is, if nothing else, a mountainous country. It lies on the boundary between three tectonic plates: the Pacific and Philippine plates beneath the Pacific Ocean and the Eurasian plate, which is predominately beneath the Asian continent. The archipelago of Japan formed to a great extent through the uplift and volcanic activity caused by those plates pushing against each other. Three quarters of the land mass of Japan resulting from that activity is mountainous with the remaining parts being inland valleys and coastal plains. As such, the image of the mountain is all-pervasive in Japanese culture, and is incorporated into all aspects of that culture from ancient religions to urban gardens.

For the people of the Heian period, mountains were primarily considered sacred places. Unlike *sato*, villages (not to mention towns or cities), *yama* was the word for a place that was not a part of people's everyday lives — a place apart. The tops of mountains were perceived as being the spots where *kami*, gods, descended when they visited the earthly plane, and, as such they were not tread on lightly. The words *hayama* (edge mountain) and *toyama* (outer mountain) referred to those parts of a mountain range that were close to human settlements but accessed only irregularly for hunting and gathering. *Miyama* (deep mountain) was the word reserved for that part of the mountains that was least accessible, most foreboding, and, perhaps, most sacred to the villagers.[202]

In Gardens

One of the cornerstones of garden making in Japan was the creation, in the abstract, of artificial mountains. The first record of a gardener in the *Nihon Shoki, Chronicles of Japan*, is in the year 612, when we find a craftsman from the Korean kingdom of Kudara (Paekche) arriving in Japan to seek his fortune. He ends up building a symbolic abstraction of Mount Sumeru, the central locus of Buddhist cosmology.[203] His mountain was most likely a carved stone sculpture, but over the years this sacred mountain has been expressed in Japanese gardens more often with a natural boulder that has been set standing vertically. Gardeners also built artificial hillocks in gardens and planted them with various trees to evoke the feeling of a mountain scene. Even though the largest of these would make hill and valley shapes large enough to stroll through, they were certainly not "mountains" by virtue of their physical size, and yet they were referred to with the word *yama* as if they were true mountains.

Both *Genji Monogatari* and *Makura no Sōshi*, which describe the residential gardens of the imperial courtiers, mention that there were *yama* in the gardens. Genji's Rokujō garden, for instance, is depicted as having had hills in the southeast planted with spring-flowering trees and more hills in the northwest covered with trees known for their fall color. It makes clear that Genji took the original hills and lake that existed there (from the previous estate and/or from its pre-capital, natural condition) and reshaped them to create the garden forms he wanted.[204] Murasaki Shikibu describes musicians playing flutes in the garden during a performance for the emperor, meandering along a path through the forested hills there.[205]

Artificial mountain forms are also described in the *Sakuteiki*. In part, the descriptions detail the scenic quality of the design, what the *Sakuteiki* authors termed *fuzei*. For instance, to create the feeling of a *yamazato*, bucolic mountain village, one would start by making a tall hill close to the residence, then pepper the face of the hill with boulders to evoke the feeling of bedrock breaking through. But the creation of mountains in the garden had other, geomantic, purposes as well. The physical shape of the land was perceived as being able to control the flow of life energy around the residence, so the correct placement of hill forms was considered life affirming and the improper placement, life threatening. For example, making hills whose valleys opened toward the house was considered unlucky for the women of the house.[206]

In Poetry

In poetry, the symbolic usages of *yama* are many and various. Like the word *no* (meadow), *yama* defined a place apart, distant, perhaps beautiful but undoubtedly wild and raw. This sense of separation from the everyday world is at times heightened in poems by the introduction into the poem of the image of *kiri* (mists) that veil the mountains from sight. There are many *makura-kotoba* related to the word *yama*. *Yamakawa no* (mountain river), as one example links to *hayashi* (quick), *oto* (sound), and *nagare* (flowing). There are also many other informal poetic associations such as *yamabiko* (mountain echo) that inks to *kotae* (answer) and *koe* (voice), and *yamagatsu* (lowly mountain folk), which is associated with any person, such as a forester or hunter, who works in the mountains. *Yamamori* (mountain warden) was used poetically as a symbol of protection, and *yamazato* (village in the mountains), was associated with either the pastoral image of a small agricultural village or, contrarily, the loneliness and desolation of such a place. As noted in the *Sakuteiki*, creating the atmosphere, *fuzei*, of a *yamazato* in gardens was a standard design theme for Heian-period gardeners. Beyond these, there are also numerous associations with particularly famous mountains, none more so than Mount Fuji that have been written about in poems since the era of the *Man'yōshū*.

There are many diverse ways in which *yama* is presented in poetry, but one can see three main trends or themes — natural beauty, spiritual journeys, and loneliness. The first group consists of those poems that revel in the seasonal beauty of the mountains, in particular spring and fall. In spring, cherries blooming in profusion are a favorite theme, seen either from afar or from the perspective of a person hunting out the blooms. In autumn, it is the rich fall colors of the forest, and the quick streams and cool winds that flow out of them, that attracted the poets. The second theme presents the *yama* as the abode of the gods or simply a place apart, to which one goes to separate oneself from the world of human civilization, a tough place, difficult to surmount or pass through, with the *yamaji* (mountain path) becoming a metaphor for the route toward spiritual enlightenment. And the third theme, at times including the words *wabishi* or *sabishi*, both of which mean sadness/loneliness, brings together images of mountains with cold winds, bellowing deer, and desolate villages of rustic dwellings (*yamazato*) to evoke feelings of loneliness.

千載和歌集 1058

前大納言公任

山に登りて志ばし行ひ志侍りける時よめる

今はとて　入りなむのちぞ　思ほゆる　山路を深み　訪ふ人もなし

ima wa tote　irinamu nochi zo　omooyuru　yamaji wo fukami　tou hito mo nashi

Senzai Wakashū 1058

Former Chief Councilor of State Fujiwara no Kintō

Composed at a time when I had entered the mountains to engage in ascetic practice

And now
　　having traveled in so far
　　　　I pause to think
How deep this mountain path can be
　　how utterly alone I am

古今和歌集　944

山里は　もののわびしき　ことこそあれ　世の憂きよりは　住みよかりけり

yamazato wa　mono no wabishiki　koto koso are　yo no uki yori wa　sumi yokarikeri

Kokin Wakashū 944

It's all so true
　　the poverty and loneliness
　　　　of this mountain village
But how much better life here
　　than amid the City's pain and sorrow

Yamabuki 山吹 Kerria

The Element

Yamabuki is the name of a shrub that grows about 1 to 2 meters (3 to 6 feet) in height and sets profuse yellow blooms on its pendulous branches in late April and May. The blooms are either five-petalled singles or, sometimes, complexly set doubles. Unlike many other plants which have been bred to produce double flowering varieties for the horticultural trade, double-flowered *yamabuki* (*yae-yamabuki*), mentioned as far back as the Heian period and perhaps as far back as the *Man'yōshū*, are apparently a naturally occurring form.[207] The botanical name of *yamabuki* is Kerria japonica and it is known in English as Japanese kerria, Japanese rose, and Japanese yellow rose. *Yamabuki* was written in two ways — 山吹 and 山振. The first translates literally as "mountains blows" and the second as "mountain trembles." Both refer to the fact that the pendulous branches move easily in the wind, something that is especially clear when they are laden with flowers. One of the common natural habitats of the *yamabuki* is along streams and rivers, and it is certainly in this light that it was remembered by poets of Japan's classical era.

Yamabuki was, along with being the name of a plant, the name of a color — naturally, a clear yellow. Although there are many references to *yamabuki* plants in gardens in Heian period literature, most of the references are to layered clothing which include a *yamabuki*-colored fabric among the layers. There is also a note in the Kochō chapter of *Genji Monogatari* of *yamabuki* branches being carried about in a golden vase by page girls (in contrast to cherry branches being displayed in a silver vase).[208] In *Makura no Sōshi*, there is a note of *yamabuki* being used as part of a headdress.[209] So we can see that *yamabuki* was part of the lives of Heian courtiers not only as a garden plant, but in many other ways as well.

In Gardens

Yamabuki is mentioned fairly often in Heian-period literature that describes garden scenes. In the Otome chapter of *Genji Monogatari*, in which the four-part Rokujō garden is described, *yamabuki* shows up as part of the southeast garden, the one Genji built for himself that featured plants that flowered in spring.[210] In the opening scene of the Kochō chapter, the garden is described in all its spring profusion — cherries still in bloom, wisteria entwining the garden corridors, water birds gliding about the lake, and kerria, pouring down the banks over the lake and reflected in the water.[211] This last image, as mentioned before, was a favorite among poets and, it would seem, garden-makers alike. In fact, in this scene in *Genji Monogatari*, upon seeing the *yamabuki*, the courtiers compose some poems on the spot about *yamabuki* reflected in the water.

Double flowering blossoms seem to have been favored. In the Maboroshi chapter of *Genji Monogatari* there are complimentary comments about how large the *yamabuki* blooms in the garden are, and in *Makura no Sōshi*, *yamabuki* blooms are included in the list of "Things that Should be Large."[212]

In Poetry

Yamabuki was, because of its natural growing environment, linked with water margins — the banks of rivers and streams, and lakes as well. Places well-known for their rivers — such as Ide, that lay to the south of the Heian capital, or Yoshino, even further south near the old capital of Nara — became *uta-makura* linked to *yamabuki*. The flowers seen reflected in the water were an important poetic motif and allowed the poet to introduce the word play of two words both pronounced *utsuroi,* the first meaning reflecting (映ろひ) and the second to changing or fading away (移ろひ). The predilection of *yamabuki* for water also explains why it is so often connected with the image of little river frogs, *kawazu,* chirping away beneath the flowering *yamabuki.*

Poetically, *yamabuki* had several symbolic uses. Naturally, it is an indicator of spring. It could also be linked to one of two expressions: *nioeru imo* (a beautiful, attractive woman) and *yamu* (to finish or to end). The first stems from the obvious fact that, the richly colored *yamabuki* was likened to a gorgeous woman, as were other beautifully flowering plants, such as cherries and wisteria. The second is a word play between the similarly sounding *yamabuki* and *yamu-naki,* the latter meaning "having no end," as in an unending love.

Another linguistic connection lies between the words *yama* (mountain, 山), *yami* (darkness, 闇), and *yomi* (黄泉). *Yomi,* which translates as "the yellow well-spring" refers to the afterworld — that place where souls go to rest. There was a related superstition in Japan, that if you look into the water in which *yamabuki* flowers are being reflected, you can see through to that other world, meet the dead, and visit with love ones who have passed away.

古今和歌集　124
　　紀貫之
　　よしの河のほとりに山ぶきのさけりけるをよめる

吉野河　岸の山吹　ふく風に　そこのかげさへ　移ろひにけり
yoshinogawa　kishi no yamabuki　fuku kaze ni　soko no kage sae　utsuroinikeri

> *Kokin Wakashū* 124
>
> > Ki no Tsurayuki
> >
> > Composed upon seeing the *yamabuki* flowering on the
> banks of the Yoshino River
>
> > Mountain winds ripple across
> > > the yellow *yamabuki* that sway over
> > > > the Yoshino River
> > Scattering even those blossoms
> > > reflected in the watery depths

万葉集　2786

山吹の　にほへる妹が　はねず色の　赤裳の姿　夢に見えつつ
yamabuki no　nioeru imo ga　hanezuiro no　akamo no sugata　ime ni mietsutsu

> *Man'yōshū* 2786
>
> Oh, that girl
> > stunning as a *yamabuki*
> > > in full bloom
> Her peach-colored robes drift
> > over and over into my dreams

Yanagi 柳 Willow

The Element

Yanagi means willow. There are several possible derivations for the name, one of which is that it stems from *ya-no-ki* (矢箆木) or the "tree for making arrow shafts," which is not impossible to imagine although arrows in Japan are typically made from a particular type of bamboo called *yadake* (矢竹, Pseudosasa japonica, arrow bamboo).

There are many species of willow in Japan, both shrub form and tree form. The willow referred to in poems, however, is most often the *shidare-yanagi* (枝垂れ柳, Salix babylonica, weeping willow) and at times the *kawa-yanagi* (川柳, Salix gracilistyla, rosegold pussy willow). *Shidare-yanagi* was imported to Japan from China sometime during the Nara period (710–784) like the *ume*, plum tree. As such, it was fancied by the people of the imperial court as an exotic plant in the early years and, also like the *ume*, by the Heian-period it had become very much a part of the lives of the Japanese people and come to be thought of as a "native" tree. The *kawa-yanagi*, the name of which translates directly as "river willow," is a shrub or small tree that grows along quick-flowing streams.

Partly because of the exotic image of the *shidare-yanagi*, and partly because of its graceful form and ease of propagation, weeping willows were planted along avenues within the capitals of Japan. The *Engishiki* (延喜式), a record of annual ceremonies compiled between 927 and 967, mentions that men were allotted to care for the willow trees along Suzaku-ōji, the main north-south avenue in the capital of Heian, and that willows were planted in the blocks surrounding Shinsen-en, the imperial garden.[213]

Willows were also used for a making a variety of goods such as chop-

227

sticks, cutting boards, and fine willow-work boxes (*yanai-bako*, 柳筥), and so became a part of people's lives in many ways. Because willows leaf out early in spring, they became emblematic of the approach of spring and, along with plums, were woven into headdresses that were worn at spring festivals.

In Gardens

Many records from the Heian period mention willows in gardens and they almost always describe them as growing along the banks of a garden pond. *Chiteiki*, the *Record of a Pond Pavilion*, an autobiographical record of the life and times of Yoshishige no Yasutane, mentions willows planted along his pond.[214] In *Genji Monogatari* there are several passages mentioning willows including one in the Sakaki chapter in which Genji visits the cloistered former-empress Fujitsubo. The season is after the New Year and he finds the pond in the garden cleared of its thin ice, hinting at a date in early spring. The willows along the bank that he sees would have been heavy with trailing stems of new buds and just sprouted leaves.[215]

The clearest description of willows in gardens, however, comes from the *Sakuteiki* that points out several aspects of the use of willows. First, it notes that willows should be used in making the Reed Style of garden which requires trees with soft and gentle forms. In another passage it suggests that willows should be planted on islands in the garden ponds, along with pine trees. It reveals that willows were used for geomantic purposes, suggesting the planting of nine willows on the east side of the garden as a substitute for the water element if a stream could not be built there. And finally, it suggests that it would be appropriate to plant a willow by the entry gate of a property belonging to a person of high standing — but only a person of such standing. Perhaps this was a linguistic connection since the pronunciation of "willow-gate," *ryū-mon*, is the same as that of "dragon-gate," a symbol of entry into the higher level of society.[216]

In Poems

In poems, *yanagi* (which at times was shortened for reasons of cadence to *yagi*) were used as an indicator of spring. Naturally. They often were introduced in the same poems as plums, another symbol of spring, especially in the *Man'yōshū* which was compiled at a time when both of those trees were relatively new imports from China.

The gracefully flowing quality of willows, especially weeping willows — with their long thread-like branches and long supple leaves — were used as metaphors for beautiful, graceful women and vice versa. Long flowing hair, for instance, which was highly prized at that time, was called *yanagi no kami* (willow hair), and eyebrows as elegantly slim as a willow leaf were known as *yanagi no mayu* (willow eyebrows), also pronounced *ryūbi*. Both of these were used as imagery in poems.

Because willows were planted as street trees in the capital, and they appeared hanging over entry gates and in gardens as well, the plant became a symbol of the capital itself and is used at times in poems that reflect on the capital.

The main symbolic use in poetry, however, was to employ the bright pale-green, newly budding or newly leafing willow as a symbol, not only of the arrival of spring, but also of new life and renewed vigor.

万葉集　825
　　小監土氏百村

梅の花　咲きたる園の　青柳を　縵にしつつ　遊び暮らさな
ume no hana　sakitaru sono no　aoyagi wo　kazura ni shitsutsu　asobi-kurasa na

　　Man'yōshū 825
　　　Shōken Hanishi no Momomura

　Come, let's gather wreaths
　　　of new green willow stems
　　　　　from the garden where plums blossom
　Wrap them into garlands for our hair
　　　and while the day away

金葉和歌集　25
　　源雅兼朝臣
　　池邊柳をよめる

風ふけば　浪のあやおる　池水に　糸ひきそふる　岸の青柳
kaze fuke ba　nami no aya oru　ikemizu ni　ito hikisouru　kishi no aoyagi

　　Kin'yō Wakashū 25
　　　Minamoto no Masakane no Ason
　　　Composed about willows growing on the edge of the
pond

　As spring winds blow
　　　waves weave patterned cloth
　　　　　across the waters of the pond
　Fed threads of new green
　　　by the willows on the banks

Yuki 雪 *Snow*

The Element

Yuki means snow, and snow itself needs little introduction, except to say that, back in the Heian period, the capital city got a generous amount through the winter months — December to February. Although the present-day city, Kyōto, gets less (due to all the urban development and associated heat mass), older residents of the city talk about how even fifty to sixty years ago the snowfall in the city was more like it still is in the hills just north of the city, where a meter (3 feet) of snow on the ground is not unusual.

In Gardens

Whether or not there was snow in Heian-period gardens is a foregone conclusion. It snows in Japan, so it snows in the gardens. The degree to which the Heian-period courtiers appreciated this snow, however, is surprising. In both *Genji Monogatari* and *Makura no Sōshi*, which describe court life in detail, scenes in which the courtiers mention how beautiful the snow is, or linger on the veranda simply to appreciate the recent snowfall, or falling snow, appear time after time.

In both books there are scenes in which courtiers, or their young attendants, go out into the garden after a heavy snowfall, roll snow into balls and pile them up to make artificial mountains.[217] This playful reaction to snow in the garden makes it clear that snowy days were not necessarily perceived as dreary or entrapping. Rather, there was a sense of delight exhibited in their actions.

In the Otome chapter of *Genji Monogatari*, in the description of the four-part garden Genji built for his four women, it is noted that in the northwestern section, which was the portion devoted to winter, pine trees grew in a thick grove, the intention of which was to show off the beauty of the snow in that season.[218] This reveals that portions of the garden were designed specifically with the thought in mind of how they would look when covered in a layer of snow.

Moonlight also figures closely with snow in both *Genji Monogatari* and *Makura no Sōshi*. We find multiple passages that describe the beauty of moonlight reflecting off the snow in the garden. There is a short section in *Makura no Sōshi* devoted to how beautiful the garden is after a light snowfall. In it a man appears at night by surprise and sits on the veranda chatting up the ladies of the court with the snowy garden as a backdrop to it all. Interestingly, Sei Shōnagon mentions that when there is a cover of snow, there is no need for a lamp at night because the snow reflects enough light inside.[219] Perhaps this is one reason why snow was so appealing to the Heian-period courtiers. Much of their social lives — their private lives, that is — was carried on at night. Spreading white sand over the garden, or having the garden covered in snow, meant that moonlight would reflect into the rooms filling them with a pleasant, natural light. At a time well before electric lights, clear, moonlit nights over a snowy garden must have been bright and "lit-up" — something to look forward to.

In Poetry

In poetry, there are many kinds of *yuki*: *shirayuki* (白雪, white snow) speaks to the clarity of things; *awayuki* (淡雪, light snow) describes the most gentle covering of snow; *hatsuyuki* (初雪, first snow), marks that day at the end of autumn of the first snowfall; *ōyuki* (おほ雪, heavy snow), from a real snow storm; *miyuki* (み雪, beautiful snow or deep snow), which always suggests beautiful snow; and, *tomomatsu yuki* (友待つ雪),

which refers to snow that lingers until the next snowfall.

Yuki is used to mark the season of winter in three distinct ways. The first is to call out the transition of autumn to winter: snow on late chrysanthemums or fallen leaves in fall color flowing in snow-swelled streams work as images this way; the second is mid-winter in which the depth of snow marks the fullness of the season; and the third is snow marking the edge of winter and spring, often expressed with tufts of snow on branches emulating spring flowers.

Yuki often appears in poems simply as part of the description of a beautiful landscape scene, but at times there is a hint of sadness, or of biding time, as winter waits for the coming of spring. Plants that are most often linked to snow in poems are *matsu* (pine tree) and *take* (bamboo) because these two evergreen plants stand in contrast to the white snow, the former usually presented as bold, strong, and upright, the latter shown bent under its weight; *unohana* (deutzia) because the brilliant white of a deutzia hedge in full bloom looks like it is heaped with snow; *kiku* (chrysanthemum), which gets tinged with color as frost and snow gather lightly on it at the end of the autumn season, or which can be mistaken for fallen snow when still white; and *ume* (plum), the flowers of which look like dabs of snow on its branches and vice versa.

Yuki can be used to express a variety of emotions: great beauty, hopefulness (as in the spring to come), or the weight of misery. Because of the similarities in the sound of the two transposed words, *yuki* (snow) and *kiyu* (disappear or melt away), the words are considered to be linked as *engo* in poetry.

紀貫之集 365
　　紀貫之
　　人の家に、女、すだれのもとに、立ち出でて、雪の木に降りかかれ
るを見る

草木にも　花咲きにけり　降る雪や　春より先に　花となるらん
kusaki ni mo　hana sakinikeri　furu yuki ya　haru yori saki ni　hana to naruran

Ki no Tsurayukishū 365
　　Ki no Tsurayuki
　　At someone's house, a woman steps out to where the
screens hang (on the veranda) and gazes over the snow falling on
the trees (of the garden)

　All the trees and grasses alike
　　　are blossoming　　could it be
　Even before the spring
　　　falling snow
　　　　　　becomes flowers in the garden

古今和歌集　329
　　凡河内みつね
　　雪のふれるを見てよめる

雪降りて　人もかよはぬ　道なれや　あとはかもなく　思ひ消ゆらむ
yuki furite　hito mo kayowanu　michi nare ya　atohaka mo naku　omoi kiyuramu

Kokin Wakashū 329
　　Ōshikōchi no Mitsune
　　Composed while watching the snow fall

Could it be　　like a path
　　which lies covered deep in snow
　　　　　untrammeled by any soul
　Like all those hidden footsteps
　　　thoughts disappear without a trace

YANAGI

kaze fuke ba
nami no aya oru
ikemizu ni
ito hikisouru
kishi no aoyagi

Kin'yō Wakashū 25

WILLOW

As spring winds blow
waves weave patterned cloth
across the waters of the pond
Fed threads of new green
by the willows on the banks

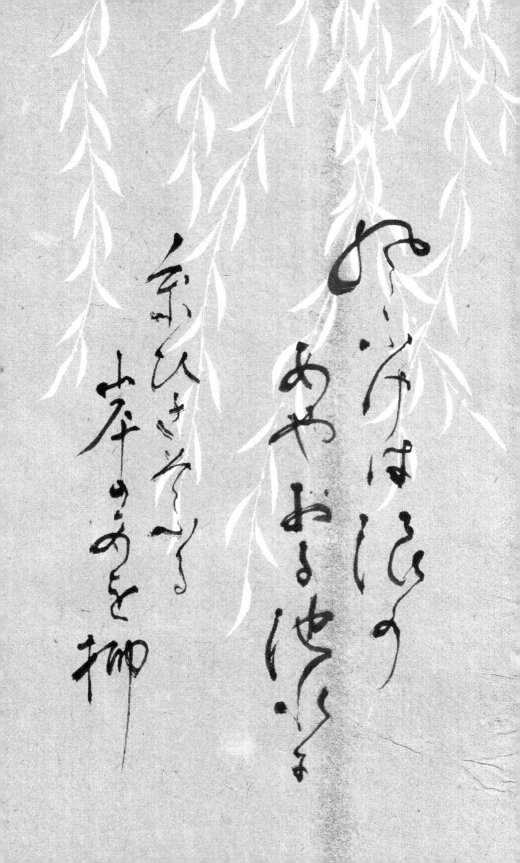

やなぎはるの
あやおるせいふ
京にさかる
岸のあをを柳

Notes

Key to Abbreviations in Notes:

NKBT > *Nihon Koten Bungaku Taikei* 日本古典文學大系

NKBZ > *Nihon Koten Bungaku Zenshū* 日本古典文學全集

SNKBT > *Shin Nihon Koten Bungaku Taikei* 新日本古典文学大系

SNKS > *Shinchō Nihon Koten Shūsei* 新潮日本古典集成

1   Tyler, pp. 657-658; SNKBT vol. 21, p. 378.

2   「やまとうたは、人の心を種として、万（よろづ）の言（こと）の葉（は）とぞなれりける、世中にある人、ことわざ繁き（しげき）ものなれば、心に思ふことを見るもの聞くものにつけて言ひ出（いだ）せるなり、花に鳴く鶯（うぐひす）、水に住む蛙（かはづ）の声（こゑ）を聞けば、生きとし生けるものいづれか歌（うた）をよまざりける」『古今和歌集』NKBZ Vol. 7, p. 49.

3   七草（七種）の節供; *nanakusa no sekku,* 7th day of the 1st month.

4   端午節会; *tango no sechie,* 5th day of the 5th month; referred to more commonly these days as *tango no sekku* 端午節句.

5   豊明節会 *toyo no akari no sechie.*

6   The rhyming word was called a *tan'in* (探韻). Tyler, pp. 155-156; SNKBT vol. 19, p. 274.

7   SNKBT, vol. 20, p. 271.

8   SNKBT, vol. 20, p. 413.

9   SNKBT, vol. 20, p. 413.

10   SNKBT, vol. 23, p. 32.

11   SNKBT, vol. 23, p. 32.

12   Morris, pp. 16-19; NKBT vol. 19, pp. 60-63.

13   Levy, pp. 358-359; NKBZ vol. 3, pp. 66-68, poem 814 preface.

14   Tyler, p. 303; SNKBT vol. 20, p. 136.

15 Kamens, *Utamakura*, p. 3.

16 NKBZ vol. 4, p. 334.

17 NKBZ vol. 2, p. 89.

18 The deceased person Kakinomoto no Hitomaro refers to in his poem is Kusakabe no Miko, who died as crown prince but was later postumously given the title of Sumeramikoto (Emperor). Karu no Miko was the son of Kusakabe and Princess Abe.

19 NKBZ vol. 7, p. 254.

20 SNKBT vol. 10, p. 354.

21 Written in reply to a poem about "making one's way home through mists" from a man who had recently returned from his service to Toshiyori who was the Governor of Shimotsufusa. This poem is an unusual *sedōka* (旋頭歌) having one extra line of 5 syllables — 5/7/5 5/7/7 — whereas most *sedōka* have one extra line of seven — 5/7/7 5/7/7.

22 NKBZ vol. 7, p. 100.

23 NKBZ vol. 7, p. 81.

24 NKBZ vol. 7, p. 357.

25 SNKBT vol. 7, p. 188.

26 The *Man'yōshū* was written in an ancient form known as *man'yōgana,* which employed Chinese characters to represent Japanese by sound not meaning. It was becoming difficult to read by the Heian period so the Office of Poetry was assigned to add pointers to the text that greatly increased its accessibility.

27 For a detailed description of how geomancy was presented in the *Sakuteiki,* see Takei & Keane, *Sakuteiki,* pp. 61-87.

28 Morris, p. 145; NKBT vol. 19, p. 195.

29 Tyler, p. 21; SNKBT vol. 19, p. 32.

30 Takei & Keane, *Sakuteiki,* p. 162; Uehara, *Sakuteiki,* p. 53.

31 Takei & Keane, *Sakuteiki,* p. 192; Uehara, *Sakuteiki,* p. 65.

32 Takei & Keane, *Sakuteiki,* p. 167; Uehara, *Sakuteiki,* p. 55.

33 NKBZ vol. 3, p. 336.

34 Morris, p. 61; NKBT vol. 19, p. 106.

35 Tyler, p. 60; SNKBT vol. 19, p. 110.

36 Tyler, p. 935; SNKBT vol. 23, p. 41.

37 Bowring, pp. 233-234; Hanawa, p. 595.

38 *Nihon Shoki* At this time a certain thing was produced between Heaven and Earth. It was in form like a reed-shoot. Now this became transformed into a God, and was called Kuni-toko-tachi no Mikoto. 『日本書紀』于時天地之中生一物。状如葦牙。便化爲神號國常立尊。"Japanese Historical Text Initiative." Berkeley Digital Library SunSITE. Web. 12 July 2010. <http://sunsite.berkeley.edu/jhti/>.

39 *Nihon Shoki* In one writing it is said: "The Gods of Heaven addressed Izanagi no Mikoto and Izanami no Mikoto, saying: 'There is the country Toyo-ashi-hara-chi-i-wo-aki no midzu-ho. Do ye proceed and bring it into order.' 『日本書紀』一書曰。天神謂伊弉諾尊 伊弉冉尊曰。 有豊葦原千五百秋瑞穂之地。宜汝往循之。"Japanese Historical Text Initiative." Berkeley Digital Library SunSITE. Web. 12 July 2010. <http://sunsite.berkeley.edu/jhti/>.

40 Takei & Keane, *Sakuteiki*, p. 165; Uehara, *Sakuteiki,* p. 54.

41 Takei & Keane, *Sakuteiki*, p. 165; Uehara, *Sakuteiki,* p. 54.

42 Tyler, p. 554; SNKBT vol. 21, pp. 164-165.

43 Tyler, p. 476; SNKBT vol. 21, p. 23.

44 Morris, pp. 44-45; NKBT vol. 19, pp. 85-87.

45 Takei & Keane, *Sakuteiki*, p. 165; Uehara, *Sakuteiki,* p. 54.

46 Tyler, p. 402; SNKBT vol. 20, p. 324.

47 *Kyōto no teien*, p. 61.

48 Tyler, p. 562; SNKBT vol. 21, p. 178.

49 Morris, p. 90; NKBT vol. 19, p. 136.

50 *Makura no Sōshi*, p. 36.

51 Tyler, p. 996; SNKBT vol. 23, p. 169.

52 *Midō Kanpakuki* 御堂関白記 was the diary of Fujiwara Michinaga, compiled between 995 and 1021; the reference to aristocrats collecting from the wild comes from the 6th day of the 9th month, 1012 (長和元年). As cited in Hida, *Heian Jidai no Shokusai*, 8.623 (1990): p. 20.

53 Morris, p. 101; NKBT vol. 19, p. 146.

54 Morris, pp. 62, 135; NKBT vol. 19, pp. 106, 184.

55 Morris, p. 62; NKBT vol. 19, p. 106.

56 *Kojiki* Thereupon, the two deities stood on the Heavenly Floating Bridge and, lowering the jeweled spear, stirred with it. They stirred the brine with a churning-churning sound; and when they lifted up [the spear] again, the brine dripping down from the tip of the spear piled up and became an island. This was

the island ONÖGÖRÖ. 『古事記』　天浮橋而。指下其沼矛以畫者。鹽許
袁呂許袁邇。畫鳴。而。引上時。自其矛末垂落之鹽。累積成嶋。淤能
碁呂嶋。"Japanese Historical Text Initiative." Berkeley Digital Library SunSITE.
Web. 12 July 2010. <http://sunsite.berkeley.edu/jhti/>.

Nihon Shoki In one writing it is said: --"The Gods of Heaven addressed Izanagi no
Mikoto and Izanami no Mikoto, saying, 'There is the country Toyo-ashi-hara-chi-
i-wo-aki no midzu-ho. Do ye proceed and bring it into order.' They then gave them
the jewel-spear of Heaven. Hereupon the two Gods stood on the floating bridge
of Heaven, and plunging down the spear, sought for land. Then upon stirring
the ocean with it, and bringing it up again, the brine which dripped from the
spear-point coagulated and became an island, which was called Ono-goro-jima.
The two gods descended, dwelt in this island, and erected there an eight-fathom
palace. They also set up the pillar of Heaven." 『日本書紀』　一書曰。天神
謂伊弉諾尊　伊弉冉尊曰。有豊葦原千五百秋瑞穗之地。宜汝往循之。廼
賜天瓊戈。於是。二神立於天上浮橋投戈求地。因畫滄海。而引舉之。
即戈鋒垂落之潮。結而爲嶋。名曰馭慮嶋。二神降居彼嶋。化作八尋之
殿。又化竪天柱。"Japanese Historical Text Initiative." Berkeley Digital Library
SunSITE. Web. 12 July 2010. <http://sunsite.berkeley.edu/jhti/>.

57　*Nihon Shoki* This year a man emigrated from Pekche whose face and body were all
flecked with white, being perhaps affected with white ringworm. People disliking
his extraordinary appearance, wished to cast him away on an island in the sea. But
this man said, "If you dislike my spotted skin, you should not breed horses or kine
in this country which are spotted with white. Moreover, I have a small talent. I
can make the figures of hills and mountains. If you kept me and made use of me,
it would be to the advantage of the country. Why should you waste me by casting
me away on an island of the sea?" Hereupon they gave ear to his words and did not
cast him away. Accordingly he was made to draw the figures of Mount Sumi and of
the Bridge of Wu in the Southern Court. The people of that time called him by the
name of Michiko no Takumi, and he was also called Shikomaro. 『日本書紀』
是歲。自百濟國有化來者。其面身皆斑白。若有白癩者乎惡其異於人。
欲棄海中嶋。然其人曰。若惡臣之斑皮者。白斑牛馬。不可畜於國中。
亦臣有小才。能構山岳之形。其留臣而用。則爲國有利。何空之棄海嶋
耶。於是聽其辭。以不棄。仍令構須彌山形。及吳橋於南庭。時人號其
人。曰路子工。亦名芝耆摩呂。"Japanese Historical Text Initiative." Berkeley

Digital Library SunSITE. Web. 12 July 2010. <http://sunsite.berkeley.edu/jhti/>.

58 Takei & Keane, *Sakuteiki*, p. 155; Uehara, *Sakuteiki,* p. 52.

59 Bowring, p. 43; SNKBT vol. 24, p. 341.

60 This poem is unusual, having one extra line of 5 syllables. See note 21.

61 *Kojiki* "Again she sang this song: In the bay of KUSAKA, grow lotuses of the bay, flowering lotuses, ah those in their prime, how I envy them." 又歌曰。久佐加延能。伊理延能波知須。波那婆知須。能佐加理毘登。登母志岐呂加母。 "Japanese Historical Text Initiative." Berkeley Digital Library SunSITE. Web. 12 July 2010. <http://sunsite.berkeley.edu/jhti/>.

62 Morris, p. 36; NKBT vol. 19, pp. 76-77; Major Captain of the Smaller Palace of the First Ward 小一條の大將.

63 Tyler p. 775; SNKBT vol. 22, p. 201.

64 Morris, p. 60; NKBT vol. 19, p. 105.

65 Morris, p. 157; NKBT vol. 19, p. 206.

66 Morris, p. 70; NKBT vol. 19, p. 114.

67 *Nihon Shoki* In one writing it is stated, "Sosa no wo no Mikoto said, 'In the region of the Land of Han there is gold and silver. It will not be well if the country ruled by my son should not possess floating riches.['] So he plucked out his beard and scattered it. Thereupon Cryptomerias were produced. Moreover, he plucked out the hairs of his breast, which became Thuyas. The hairs of his buttocks became Podocarpi. The hairs of his eye-brows became Camphor-trees. Having done so, he determined their uses. These two trees, viz. the Cryptomeria and the Camphor-tree, were to be made into floating riches; the Thuya was to be used as timber for building fair palaces; the Podocarpus was to form receptacles in which the visible race of man was to be laid in secluded burial-places.["] 一書曰。素戔鳴尊曰。韓郷之嶋。是有金銀。若使吾兒所御之國。不有浮寶者。未是佳也。乃拔鬚髯散之。即成杉。又拔散胸毛。是成檜。尻毛是成柀。眉毛是成樟。已而定其當用。乃稱之曰。杉及樟。此兩樹者。可以爲浮寶。檜可以爲瑞宮之材。柀可以爲顯見蒼生。奥津棄戸。將臥之具。 "Japanese Historical Text Initiative." Berkeley Digital Library SunSITE. Web. 12 July 2010. <http://sunsite.berkeley.edu/jhti/>.

68 Takei & Keane, *Sakuteiki*, p. 196; Uehara, *Sakuteiki,* p. 67.

69 Morris, p. 46; NKBT vol. 19, p. 88.

70 Morris, p. 93; NKBT vol. 19, p. 138.

71 *Hibara* literally means *hinoki* field rather than *hinoki* forest.

72 Uraki, p. 246.

73 Tyler, p. 456; SNKBT vol. 20, p. 429.

74 Tyler, pp. 37, 775; SNKBT vol. 19, p. 62 & vol. 4, pp. 201-202.

75 *Nihon Shoki* Central Land of Reed-Plains. But in that Land there were numerous Deities which shone with a lustre like that of fireflies, and evil Deities which buzzed like flies. 『日本書紀』以爲葦原中國之主。然彼地多有螢火光神。及蠅聲邪神。 "Japanese Historical Text Initiative." Berkeley Digital Library SunSITE. Web. 12 July 2010. <http://sunsite.berkeley.edu/jhti/>.

76 The poem that refers to "burning with a single remembrance" is number 3984 from the *Kokin Rokujō*.

77 Bowring, p. 123; SNKBT vol. 24, p. 304. Morris, p. 48; NKBT vol. 19, p. 91.

78 Tyler, pp. 223-224; SNKBT vol. 19, p. 396. Tyler, pp. 1054-1055; SNKBT VOL. 23, p. 280.

79 *Nihon Shoki* Agriculture is the great foundation of the Empire. It is that upon which the people depend for their subsistence. At present the water of Hanida of Sayama in Kahachi is scarce, and therefore the peasants of that province are remiss in their husbandry. Open up therefore abundance of ponds and runnels, and so develop the industry of the people. Winter, 10th month. The Yosami pond was made. 11th month. The Karusaka pond and the Sakahori pond were made. One version has: These three ponds were made when the Emperor dwelt in the Palace of Kuhama. 『日本書紀』農天下之大本也。民所恃以生也。今河内狭山埴田水少。是以其國百姓怠於農事。其多開池溝。以寛民業。冬十月。造依網池。十一月。作苅坂池。反折池。一云。天皇居桑間宮。造是三池也。 "Japanese Historical Text Initiative." Berkeley Digital Library SunSITE. Web. 12 July 2010. <http://sunsite.berkeley.edu/jhti/>. Note: the historical records in the *Nihon Shoki* before the 7th century are not considered highy accurate.

80 *Nihon Shoki* Summer, 5th month, 20th day. The Oho-omi died. He was buried in the tomb at Momohara. The Oho-omi was the son of Iname no Sukune. He had a talent for military tactics, and was also gifted with eloquence. He reverenced deeply the Three Precious Things. His house stood on the bank of the river Asuka. A small pond had been dug in the courtyard, and there was a little island in the middle of the pond. Therefore the men of that time called him Shima no Oho-omi. 『日本書紀』夏五月戊子朔丁未。大臣薨。仍葬于桃原墓。大臣則稲目

宿禰之子也。性有武略。亦有辨才。以恭敬三寶。家於飛鳥河之傍。乃庭中開小池。仍興小嶋於池中。故時人曰嶋大臣。"Japanese Historical Text Initiative." Berkeley Digital Library SunSITE. Web. 12 July 2010. <http://sunsite.berkeley.edu/jhti/>. Soga no Umako (蘇我馬子: 551?–June 19, 626).

81   Water Level device: Takei & Keane, *Sakuteiki*, p. 157; Uehara, *Sakuteiki*, p. 52.

water height: Takei & Keane, *Sakuteiki*, p. 157; Uehara, *Sakuteiki*, p. 52.

set stones: Takei & Keane, *Sakuteiki*, p. 157; Uehara, *Sakuteiki*, p. 52.

water flow: Takei & Keane, *Sakuteiki*, pp. 158, 194; Uehara, *Sakuteiki*, pp. 52, 66.

pond edges soft: Takei & Keane, *Sakuteiki*, p. 166; Uehara, *Sakuteiki*, p. 55.

pond edge: Takei & Keane, *Sakuteiki*, p. 166; Uehara, *Sakuteiki*, p. 55.

shallow (for fish) : Takei & Keane, *Sakuteiki*, p. 192; Uehara, *Sakuteiki,* p. 66.

water fowl: Takei & Keane, *Sakuteiki*, p. 192; Uehara, *Sakuteiki*, p. 66.

water shape: Takei & Keane, *Sakuteiki*, p. 192; Uehara, *Sakuteiki,* p. 65.

82   lotuses on surface: Tyler, p. 657; SNKBT vol. 21, p. 378.

slicked with ice: Tyler, p. 373; SNKBT vol. 20, p. 268.

willows overhang the banks: Tyler, p. 214; SNKBT vol. 19, p. 380.

flocks of waterfowl: Tyler, p. 442; SNKBT vol. 20, p. 401.

choked with weeds: Tyler, p. 65; SNKBT vol. 19, p. 120.

moonlight: Tyler, p. 234; SNKBT vol. 20, pp. 13-14.

musicians in Chinese-style boats: Tyler, p. 441; SNKBT vol. 20, p. 401.

cool air above the water: Tyler, p. 1063; SNKBT vol. 23, p. 298.

cormorant fisher: Tyler, p. 573; SNKBT vol. 21, p. 196.

83   Morris, pp. 172, 174; NKBT vol. 19, pp. 221, 224.

84   Takei & Keane, *Sakuteiki*, p. 183; Uehara, *Sakuteiki*, p. 62.

85   Takei & Keane, *Sakuteiki*, p. 175; Uehara, *Sakuteiki,* pp. 58-59.

86   Takei & Keane, *Sakuteiki*, p. 191; Uehara, *Sakuteiki,* pp. 64-65.

87   Takei & Keane, *Sakuteiki*, p. 188; Uehara, *Sakuteiki*, p. 63.

88   Stones in streams: Tyler, pp. 275, 402, 998; SNKBT vol. 20, pp. 87, 323, vol. 23, p. 155.

Stones in island cove: Tyler, p. 441; SNKBT vol. 20, p. 401.

89   Morris, p. 42; NKBZ vol. 11, p. 126 (this passage is not found in the NKBT edition).

90   Tyler, pp. 402, 445; SNKBT vol. 20, pp. 323, 405.

91   Tyler, p. 402; SNKBT vol. 20, p. 324.

92   Morris, p. 235; NKBT vol. 19, 302.

93   *shibagaki* 柴垣: Tyler, p. 37; SNKBT vol. 19, p. 62.

       ueshi no kakine 植ゑし垣根: Tyler, p. 224; SNKBT vol. 19, p. 396.

       take ameru kaki 竹編める垣: Tyler, p. 250; SNKBT vol. 20, p. 41.

       kuroki akagi no magaki 黒木赤木の籬: Tyler, p. 487; SNKBT vol. 21, p. 36.

       kuretake no magaki 呉竹の籬: Tyler, p. 541; SNKBT vol. 21, p. 142.

94   *Man'yōshū*　「やすみしし　わご大君の　高知（たかし）らす　吉野の宮
       は　たたなづく　青垣こもり」『万葉集　923』NKBZ vol. 3, p. 136.

       Kojiki　He replied, saying:"Worship me on the eastern mountain of the verdant
       fence of YAMATÖ." This is the deity who dwells on Mount MI-MÖRÖ.『古
       事記』荅言吾者。伊都岐奉于倭之青垣東山上。此者坐御諸山上神
       也。"Japanese Historical Text Initiative." Berkeley Digital Library SunSITE. Web.
       12 July 2010. <http://sunsite.berkeley.edu/jhti/>.

95   Tyler, p. 633; SNKBT vol. 21, p. 323.

96   Harris, p. 35; NKBZ vol. 8, p. 133.　Tyler, p. 86; SNKBT vol. 19, p. 157.

97   Takei & Keane, *Sakuteiki*, p. 165; Uehara, *Sakuteiki,* p. 54.

98   Harris, p. 45; NKBZ vol. 8, p. 140.

99   Tyler, pp. 130-131; SNKBT vol. 19, p. 234.

100   Tyler, p. 103; SNKBT vol. 19, p. 187.

101   Morris, p. 68; NKBT vol. 19, p. 113.

102   *Nihon Shoki*　[AD485] 3rd month, 1st day of the Serpent1 (the 2nd). The Emperor
       went to the Park, and there held revel by the winding streams. [AD486] 2nd
       year, Spring, 3rd month, 1st day of the Serpent (2nd) The Emperor went to the
       Park, where he held revel by the winding streams. At this time he assembled in
       great numbers the Ministers, the High Officials, the Omi, the Muraji, the Kuni
       no Miyakko, and the Tomo no Miyakko, and made revel. The Ministers uttered
       reiterated cries of Long live the Emperor. [AD487] 3rd month, 1st day of the
       Serpent (8th). The Emperor went to the Park, where he held revel by the winding
       streams.『日本書紀』[AD485]　三月上巳。幸後苑。曲水宴。 [AD486]　二
       年春三月上巳。幸後苑。曲水宴。是時盛集公卿大夫臣連國造伴造。
       爲宴。群臣頻稱萬歳。[AD487]　三月上巳。幸後苑。曲水宴。"Japanese
       Historical Text Initiative." Berkeley Digital Library SunSITE. Web. 12 July 2010.
       <http://sunsite.berkeley.edu/jhti/>.

103   Takei & Keane, *Sakuteiki*, pp. 175-183; Uehara, *Sakuteiki,* pp. 59-62.

104 Takei & Keane, *Sakuteiki*, pp. 164-165, 182; Uehara, *Sakuteiki,* pp. 53-54, 61.

105 Although *Genji Monogatari* is a fictional account, it is interesting that the most effete Prince Genji would strip off his outer coat and engage in that sort of work (not the cleaning, of course, but the supervision). That this would be included in the story without seeming laughable shows that this sort of direct involvement in the work of the garden was considered apropos to Heian courtiers, even for people of high rank. Tyler, pp. 338, 571; SNKBT vol. 20, p. 201; vol. 21, p. 194. Bowring, pp. 45, 57; SNKBT vol. 24, pp. 254, 262.

106 Amanogawa is the Milky Way but also the river of events that the heavens dictate, which control the lives of people on earth.

107 Water from streams was supplemented by water from springs and wells that were tapped into on individual properties.

108 NKBZ vol.7, p, 49.

109 The modern names of these three plants are most likely as follows: *momoyo-gusa* (百世草) is *nojigiku* (野路菊), Chrysanthemum occidentali-japonense; *uhagi* (薺蒿) is *yomena* (嫁菜), Kalimeris yomena; and *kawara-yomogi* (河原艾) is perhaps still *kawara-yomogi*, Artemisia capillaris.

110 Festival of Chrysanthemums, *chōyō no sechie* (重陽の節会). Tyler, p. 776; SNKBT vol. 22, p. 203. Bowring, p. 49; SNKBT vol. 24, p. 257.

111 *Kaifūsō* 懐風藻 was compiled around 751. Nagaya-ō 長屋王 (684–729) was the grandson of Emperor Tenmu. The poem includes the expression *fukiku no shu* (浮菊酒) as cited in *Koten Bungaku Shokubutsushi*, p. 128.

112 SNKBT, p. 273.

113 Takei & Keane, *Sakuteiki*, p. 167; Uehara, *Sakuteiki,* p. 55.

114 Takei & Keane, *Sakuteiki*, p. 193; Uehara, *Sakuteiki,* p. 65.

115 Tyler, p. 404; SNKBT vol. 20, pp. 325-326.

116 Tyler, p. 441; SNKBT vol. 20, p. 400.

117 Tyler, p. 443; SNKBT vol. 20, p. 402.

118 Tyler, p. 1059; SNKBT vol. 23, p. 290.

119 'Covered in moss,' *koke oi* 苔生ひ, *koke musu* 苔むす.

120 NKBZ vol. 7, p. 168.

121 Morris, p. 78; NKBT vol. 19, p. 122.

122 Takei & Keane, *Sakuteiki*, p. 167; Uehara, *Sakuteiki,* p. 55.

123 Takei & Keane, *Sakuteiki*, p. 197; Uehara, *Sakuteiki,* p. 68.

124 Tyler, pp. 308, 818; SNKBT vol. 20, p. 146; vol. 22, p. 276; Morris, pp. 90, 171; NKBT vol. 19, p. 136. NKBZ vol. 11, p. 318 (the passage about a pine strangled by a wisteria vine is not found in the NKBT edition).

125 McCullough, pp. 445-446; NKBT vol. 75, p. 380.

126 Morris, p. 195; NKBT vol. 19, p. 258.

127 Normally the Fishing Pavilion is called Tsuri-dono (釣殿) but in this instance was called a Tsuri-dai (釣台). *Bunka Shūreishū* 文華秀麗集 and *Shoku Nihon Kōki* 続日本後紀, as cited in Hida, *Heian Jidai no Shokusai*, 5.620 (1990): pp. 38-39.

128 Tyler, p. 337; SNKBT vol. 20, p. 198.

129 Takei & Keane, *Sakuteiki*, p. 197; Uehara, *Sakuteiki*, p. 68.

130 Tyler, p. 402; SNKBT vol. 20, pp. 323-324.

131 The deceased person refered in his poem is Kusakabe no Miko. See note 18.

132 Emperor Konoe (1139–1155, r. 1142–1155).

133 Morris, pp. 49-50; NKBT vol. 19, pp. 92-93.

134 Tyler, p. 490; SNKBT vol. 21, p. 43.

135 Tyler, p. 712; SNKBT vol. 22, p. 75.

136 Tyler, pp. 775, 490, 402; SNKBT, vol. 22, p. 201, vol. 21, p. 43, vol. 20, p. 323.

137 Akiyama *p. 341*. In the *Kojiki*, the god of the mountains was called Ohoyamatsumi-no-kami 大山津見神, and the god of the plains/meadow was Kaya-no-hime-no-kami 鹿屋野比売神, also known as Nozuchi-no-kami 野椎神.

138 Morris, pp. 62, 125; NKBT vol. 19, p. 106. NKBZ vol. 11, p. 250 (autumn fields is not included in the list of of *awarenaru mono* found in the NKBT edition).

139 The word *nosuji* is used only in relation to gardens. It appears in the *Sakuteiki*, and in medieval poetry critiques and anthologies in poems related to gardens. An example of the former is *Renga Kokorozuke no Koto* (1476, 連歌心付之事) and of the latter is *Shūgyokushū* (1346, 拾玉集).

140 Takei & Keane, *Sakuteiki*, 167; Uehara, *Sakuteiki*, p. 55.

141 Takei & Keane, *Sakuteiki*, 183; Uehara, *Sakuteiki*, p. 61.

142 *Numaike no yō* (沼池の様) translates literally as the "marsh-pond style."

143 Takei & Keane, *Sakuteiki*, p. 165; Uehara, *Sakuteiki*, p. 54.

144 *Komori numa* (隠り沼) becomes *kakure numa* (隠れ沼).

145 Takei & Keane, *Sakuteiki*, p. 183; Uehara, *Sakuteiki*, p. 61.

146 Tyler, pp. 935, 1086; SNKBT vol. 23, pp. 41, 342.

147 Morris, p. 185; NKBT vol. 19, p. 243.

148 Bowring, pp. 45, 241; SNKBT vol. 24, pp. 254, 346.

149 *Eshi* or *heshi* (圧) means to overwhelm. There is as well another related flower called *otokoeshi*, Patrinia villosa, *otoko* being the word for "man."

150 Sakizawa (先澤) and Sakino (佐紀野).

151 Morris, p. 45; NKBT vol. 19, p. 87.

152 Takei & Keane, *Sakuteiki*, p. 200; Uehara, *Sakuteiki,* p. 68.

153 In addition to strips of white mulberry cloth, the accounts in the *Chronicles of Japan* describe cascades of jewels, called *magatama*, and even bronze mirrors being hung from these sacred branches. *Nihon Shoki* One writing says Ma-futsu no Kagami. On its lower branches they hung blue soft offerings and white soft offerings. Then they recited their liturgy together. 『日本書紀』一云。眞經津鏡。下枝懸青和幣。白和幣。相與致其祈祷焉。"Japanese Historical Text Initiative." Berkeley Digital Library SunSITE. Web. 12 July 2010. <http://sunsite.berkeley.edu/jhti/>.

154 The nomenclature of cherries is famously difficult to determine, resulting in many synonyms. Prunus serrulata is commonly referred to in most Japanese botanical dictionaries as Prunus jamasakura.

155 In front of the main hall in the imperial palace, known as Shishinden, are planted two trees, flanking the main stairs that lead up from the courtyard into the building in the center of the southern façade. A ying and yang arrangement, one tree is deciduous and the other is evergreen. The former, which is to the east side of the stairs, was a plum and became a cherry (*sakon no sakura*) and the latter, which is planted to the west of the stairs, is a citrus tree (*ukon no tachibana*). *Nihon Sandai Jitsuroku* 日本三代実録 as cited in Hida, *Heian Jidai no Shokusai*, 5.620 (1990): p. 40.

156 As cited in Hida, *Heian Jidai no Shokusai*, 7.622 (1990): p. 27.

157 *Kanke Bunsō* 菅家文草 is a collection of Chinese-style poetry compiled in the year 900 by Sugawara no Michizane; the reference to replacing cherries is in scroll five. NKBT vol. 72, pp. 408-409.

158 Also called *kaniwa-zakura* (樺桜), which may be the old name for *uwamizu-zakura*, Prunus grayana, the Japanese bird cherry. Tyler, p. 770; SNKBT vol. 22, p. 192.

159 Morris, p. 185; NKBT vol. 19, p. 243.

160 Morris, pp. 4, 15; NKBT vol. 19, pp. 46, 58-59. Bowring, p. 228; SNKBT vol. 24, p. 335.

161 Present-day mythology focuses on the "eight islands" but the actual record in the *Nihon Shoki* mentions three additional islands: Koshi, Oho-shima, and Kibi. "Now when the time of birth arrived, first of all the island of Ahaji was reckoned as the placenta, and their minds took no pleasure in it. Therefore it received the name of Ahaji no Shima. Next there was produced the island of Oho-yamato no Toyo-aki-tsu-shima. Next they produced the island of Iyo no futa-na, and next the island of Tsukushi. Next the islands of Oki and Sado were born as twins. This is the prototype of the twin-births which sometimes take place among mankind. Next was born the island of Koshi, then the island of Oho-shima, then the island of Kibi no Ko. Hence first arose the designation of the Oho-ya-shima country. Then the islands of Tsushima and Iki, with the small islands in various parts, were produced by the coagulation of the foam of the salt-water." 『日本書紀』及至産時。先以淡路洲爲胞。意所不快。故名之曰淡路洲。廼生大日本。[日本。此云耶麻騰。下皆效此。] 豐秋津洲。次生伊豫二名洲。次生筑紫洲。次雙生億岐洲。與佐度洲。世人或有雙生者。象此也。次生越洲。次生大洲。次生吉備子洲。由是始起大八洲國之號焉。即對馬嶋。壹岐嶋。及處處小嶋。皆是潮沫凝成者矣。 Japanese Historical Text Initiative." Berkeley Digital Library SunSITE. Web. 12 July 2010. <http://sunsite.berkeley.edu/jhti/>.

162 *Shimazutau* (島伝ふ), "going along the islands."

163 Banishing someone to an island is now known as *shima-nagashi* (島流し), literally float someone off to an island, but in *The Chronicles of Japan* the expression *kikaitō* (棄海嶋) was used.

164 Tyler, pp. 400, 441; SNKBT vol. 20, pp. 319, 400-401.

165 Takei & Keane, *Sakuteiki*, pp. 157-58, 167-68; Uehara, *Sakuteiki*, pp. 52.

166 Takei & Keane, *Sakuteiki*, pp. 155, 167-68; Uehara, *Sakuteiki*, pp. 51-52, 55-56.

167 Tyler, p. 107; SNKBT vol. 19, p. 195.

168 Morris, p. 1; NKBT vol. 19, p. 43.

169 In *Senzai Wakashū* 397, an reference to frost and temple bells is made. This draws from a legend that in China, at a temple on Mount Buzan (豊山), the light frost of a cold morning actually made the temple bell ring itself. The image is beautiful, but also evokes a sense of profound cold and loneliness.

170 *Noki-shinobu* (roof-eave fern, 軒しのぶ), *yatsume-ran* (many-eyed orchid, 八つ目蘭).

171 Tyler, p. 830; SNKBT vol. 22, p. 300.

172   Tyler, pp. 64, 311; SNKBT vol. 19, p. 118, vol. 20, p. 151.

173   Morris, p. 60; NKBT vol. 19, p. 105.

174   Tyler, p. 571; SNKBT vol. 21, p. 194.

175   Tyler, p. 691; SNKBT vol. 22, p. 39.

176   Yamatoji (大和道) and Urano (宇良野).

177   The word *take* is pronounced *tah-keh* now, but was pronounced *taka* in the classical eras.

178   *Suigai* is also pronounced *suigaki* (透垣), literally, see-through fence.

179   Takei & Keane, *Sakuteiki*, p. 202; Uehara, *Sakuteiki*, p. 69.

180   Takei & Keane, *Sakuteiki*, p. 178; Uehara, *Sakuteiki,* p. 60.

181   Takei & Keane, *Sakuteiki*, p. 165; Uehara, *Sakuteiki,* p. 54.

182   Tyler, p. 448; SNKBT vol. 20, p. 413.

183   Morris, pp. 142, 146; NKBT vol. 19, p. 197.

184   Nachi no Taki (那智の滝), Hirō Jinja (飛瀧神社).

185   Fudō Myōō (不動明王), Acala in Sanskrit.

186   Takei & Keane, *Sakuteiki*, pp. 169-175; Uehara, *Sakuteiki,* pp. 56-59.

187   NKBT vol. 9, p. 58. *Taketori Monogatari* (竹取物語), *The Tale of the Bamboo Cutter*, is also known as *Kaguya Hime* (かぐや姫), *The Tale of Princess Kaguya.*

188   Tyler, p. 939; SNKBT vol. 23, p. 50.

189   Tyler, pp. 641-642; SNKBT vol. 21, p. 341.

190   Tyler, p. 490; SNKBT vol. 21, p. 43.

191   The floss silk on the chrysanthemum was called *kiku no kisewata*. It was associated with the evening before the 9th day of the 9th month festival, and had the additional purpose of keeping the flowers safe from the frost before the important day.

192   Morris, pp. 13 (*kiku*), 42 (*hagi*), 42 (*sakura*), 125 (*asaji*), 135 (*kumo*), 149 (*grass*); NKBT vol. 19, pp. 55 (菊), 83 (櫻), 83 (萩), 171 (浅茅), 184 (蜘蛛の巣), 199 (御前の草).

193   Which plant *asagao* refers to is not clearly determined. For a description see the entry on *asagao*.

194   Morris, p. 48; NKBT vol. 19, p. 90.

195   Tyler, p. 769; vol. 22, p. 191.

196   See footnote number 155 from entry on *sakura*.

197   *Kyōto no teien*, p. 61.

198   Morris, p. 76; NKBT vol. 19, p. 120.

199 Tyler, pp. 436, 638; SNKBT vol. 20. p. 387, vol. 21, pp. 333-334.

200 Tyler, p. 402; SNKBT vol. 20, p. 323.

201 Morris, pp. 42, 106, 193; NKBZ vol. 11, p. 126, 222, 350.

202 The word *satoyama* (village mountain) refers to that area of the mountains that is closest to human habitation and, in some part, maintained for human life. Although this concept may have existed in the Heian period, the word itself is more recent.

203 The gardener from Pekche was named Michiko no Takumi. See note 57.

204 Tyler, p. 402; SNKBT vol. 20, p. 323.

205 Bowring, pp. 81-83; SNKBT vol. 24, pp. 277-278.

206 Takei & Keane, *Sakuteiki*, pp. 161, 190; Uehara, *Sakuteiki*, pp. 53, 64.

207 The poem in the *Man'yōshū*, number 1860, does not mention a double flowering *yamabuki* directly, but does mention a *yamabuki* with no seeds, which is true of the double flowering plant.

208 Tyler, p. 444; SNKBT vol. 20, p. 405.

209 Morris, p. 191; NKBT vol. 19, p. 252.

210 Tyler, p. 402; SNKBT vol. 20, p. 323.

211 Tyler, p. 442; SNKBT vol. 20, pp. 401-402.

212 "Things that Should be Large" is expressed *ōki nite yoki mono* (おほきにてよきもの).

213 As cited in Hida, *Heian Jidai no Shokusai*, 5.620 (1990): pp. 37-38.

214 Watson, p. 61; SNKBT vol. 39, p. 39.

215 Tyler, 214; SNKBT vol. 19, p. 380.

216 Takei & Keane, *Sakuteiki*, pp. 165, 196-197, 200; Uehara, *Sakuteiki*, pp. 54, 67-68.

217 Tyler, p. 373; SNKBT vol. 20, p. 269. Morris, p. 83; NKBT vol. 19, pp. 128-129.

218 Tyler, p. 402; SNKBT vol. 20, p. 324.

219 Morris, pp. 176-177; NKBT vol. 19, p. 227.

Bibliography

Books in English

Aston, W. G., trans. *Nihongi: Chronicles of Japan from the Earliest Times to A.D. 697*. Rutland, VT: C. E. Tuttle, 1972. (Originally published in 1896.)

Bowring, Richard, trans. *Murasaki Shikibu: Her Diary and Poetic Memoirs*. Princeton, NJ: Princeton University Press, 1982.

Carter, Steven D. *Traditional Japanese Poetry: An Anthology*. Stanford, CA: Stanford University Press, 1991.

Harris, Henry Jay, trans. *The Tales of Ise*. Rutland, VT: C. E. Tuttle, 1972.

Honda, Heihachirō, trans. *The Sanka Shū*. Tōkyō: The Hokuseido Press, 1971.

Kamens, Edward. *Utamakura, Allusion, and Intertextuality in Traditional Japanese Poetry*. New Haven, CT: Yale University Press, 1997.

Kudo, Shigenori, trans. *Gosen Wakashū*. Osaka: Izumi Shoin, 1992.

Kuitert, Wybe. *Themes in the History of Japanese Garden Art*. Honolulu, HI: University of Hawai'i, 2002.

Levy, Ian Hideo, trans. *The Ten Thousand Leaves: A Translation of the Man'yōshū, Japan's Premier Anthology of Classical Poetry*. Princeton, NJ: Princeton University Press, 1981.

McCullough, Helen Craig. *Brocade by Night: Kokin Wakashū and the Court Style in Japanese Classical Poetry*. Stanford, CA: Stanford University Press, 1985.

McCullough, William H. and Helen Craig McCullough, trans. *A Tale of Flowering Fortunes: Annals of Japanese Aristocratic Life in the Heian Period. Vol. 1 & 2*. Stanford, CA: Stanford University Press, 1980.

Morris, Ivan, trans. *The Pillowbook of Sei Shōnagon. Vol. 1* [Pillowbook] *& Vol. 2* [Notes]. New York: Columbia University Press, 1967.

Richardson, Donald M., trans. *The Anthology of a Thousand Years of Japanese Poetry*. Winchester, VA, 1997.

Rodd, Laurel Rasplica, trans. *Kokinshū: A Collection of Poems Ancient and Modern*. Princeton, NJ: Princeton University Press, 1984.

Seidensticker, Edward. *The Gossamer Years: A Diary of a Noblewoman of Heian Japan*. Tokyo: C. E. Tuttle, 1973.

Smits, Ivo. *The Pursuit of Loneliness: Chinese and Japanese Nature Poetry in Medieval Japan, Ca. 1050–1150*. Stuttgart: F. Steiner, 1995.

Takei, Jirō, and Marc Peter Keane. *Sakuteiki, Visions of the Japanese Garden*. Tokyo: Tuttle, 2008.

Tyler, Royall, trans. *The Tale of Genji*. New York: Viking, 2001.

Uraki, Jirō, trans. *The Tale of the Cavern*. Tokyo: Shinozaki Shorin, 1984.

Watson, Burton, trans. *Japanese Literature in Chinese. Vol. 1.* New York: Columbia University Press, 1975.

Books in Japanese

Abe, Manzō and Takeshi Abe, eds. *Makura-kotoba Jiten*. Tōkyō: Takashina Shoten, 1989. 阿部萬藏, 阿部猛編『枕詞辞典』東京: 高科書店.

Akiyama, Ken, ed. *Ōchōgo Jiten*. Tōkyō: Tōkyō Daigaku Shuppankai, 2000. 秋山虔編『王朝語辞典』東京: 東京大学出版会.

Fukui, Kyūzō, and Tokuhei Yamagishi. *Makura-kotoba no Kenkyū to Shakugi*, Tōkyō: Yūseidō Shuppan, 1960. 福井久藏, 山岸德平『枕詞の研究と釋義』東京: 有精堂出版.

Hanawa, Hokiichi. *Gunsho Ruijū: Vol. 15 Waka* [includes *Murasaki Shikibu Shū*], Tōkyō: Zoku Gunsho Ruijū Kanseikai, 1931. 塙 保己一『群書類従　第15輯:和歌［紫式部集を含む］』東京 : 続群書類従完成會.

Hayashi, Yasaka. *Nihon No Jumoku*. Tōkyō: Yama to Keikokusha, 1985. 林弥栄『日本の樹木』東京: 山と溪谷社.

Hida, Norio. "Teien Shokusai No Rekishi: Heian Jidai no Shokusai 1." *Nihon Bijustu Kōgei* 5.620 (1990): 36-42. 飛田範夫『庭園植栽の歴史　平安の植栽１』日本美術工芸 5.620.

Hida, Norio. "Teien Shokusai No Rekishi: Heian Jidai no Shokusai 2." *Nihon Bijustu Kōgei* 6.621 (1990): 20-26. 飛田範夫『庭園植栽の歴史　平安の植栽２』日本美術工芸 6.621.

Hida, Norio. "Teien Shokusai No Rekishi: Heian Jidai no Shokusai 3." *Nihon Bijustu Kōgei* 7.622 (1990): 26-31. 飛田範夫『庭園植栽の歴史　平安の植栽３』日本美術工芸 7.622.

Hida, Norio. "Teien Shokusai No Rekishi: Heian Jidai no Shokusai 4." *Nihon Bijustu Kōgei* 8.623 (1990): 20-26. 飛田範夫『庭園植栽の歴史　平安の植栽４』日本美術工芸　8.623.

Katagiri, Yōichi. *Utamakura Utakotoba Jiten*. Tōkyō: Kadokawa Shoten, 1983. 片桐洋一『歌枕歌ことば辞典』東京: 角川書店.

Koten Bungaku Shokubutsushi. Tōkyō: Gakutōsha, 2002.『古典文学植物誌』東京: 學燈社.

Kyōto no Teien: Iseki ni Miru Heian Jidai no Teien. Kyōto: Kyōto-shi Bunka Kankōkyoku Bunkabu Bunkazai Hogoka, 1990. 『京都の庭園: 遺跡にみる平安時代の庭園』京都: 京都市文化観光局文化部文化財保護課.

Nihon Koten Bungaku Taikei, Vol. 19 (Makura no Sōshi, Murasaki Shikibu Nikki). Tōkyō: Iwanami Shoten, 1958.『日本古典文學大系 19（枕草子, 紫式部日記）』東京: 岩波書店.

Nihon Koten Bungaku Taikei, Vol. 20 (Tosa Nikki, Kagerō Nikki, Izumi Shikibu Nikki, Sarashina Nikki). Tōkyō: Iwanami Shoten, 1957.『日本古典文學大系　20（土佐日記、蜻蛉日記、紫式部日記）』東京: 岩波書店.

Nihon Koten Bungaku Taikei, Vol. 21 (Ōkagami). Tōkyō: Iwanami Shoten, 1960.『日本古典文學大系 21（大鏡）』東京: 岩波書店.

Nihon Koten Bungaku Taikei, Vol. 29 (Sankashū, Kinkai Wakashū). Tōkyō: Iwanami Shoten, 1961.『日本古典文學大系 29（山家集, 金槐和歌集）』東京: 岩波書店.

Nihon Koten Bungaku Taikei, Vol. 69 (Kaifūsō, Bunka Shūreishū, Honchō Monzui). Tōkyō: Iwanami Shoten, 1964.『日本古典文學大系 69（懷風藻, 文華秀麗集, 本朝文粹）』東京: 岩波書店.

Nihon Koten Bungaku Taikei, Vol. 75-76 (Eiga Monogatari 1 & 2). Tōkyō: Iwanami Shoten, 1965.『日本古典文學大系 75-76（榮花物語　上下）』東京: 岩波書店.

Nihon Koten Bungaku Zenshū, Vol. 2-5 (Man'yōshū Vol. 1-4). Tōkyō: Shōgakukan, 1971–1975. 『日本古典文學全集 2～5 （万葉集 1～4）』東京：小学館.

Nihon Koten Bungaku Zenshū, Vol. 7 (Kokin Wakashū). Tōkyō: Shōgakukan, 1971. 『日本古典文學全集 7 （古今和歌集）』東京：小学館.

Nihon Koten Bungaku Zenshū, Vol. 8 (Taketori Monogatari, Ise Monogatari, Yamato Monogatari, Heichū Monogatari). Tōkyō: Shōgakukan, 1972. 『日本古典文學全集 8 （竹取物語, 伊勢物語, 大和物語, 平中物語 ）』東京：小学館.

Nihon Koten Bungaku Zenshū, Vol. 11 (Makura no Sōshi). Tōkyō: Shōgakukan, 1974. 『日本古典文學全集 11 （枕草子）』東京：小学館.

Nihon Koten Bungaku Zenshū, Vol. 20 (Ōkagami). Tōkyō: Shōgakukan, 1974. 『日本古典文學全集 20 （大鏡）』東京：小学館.

Ōno, Susumu, Akihiro Satake, and Kingorō Maeda, eds. *Iwanami Kogo Jiten*. Tōkyō: Iwanami Shoten, 1974. 大野晋, 佐竹昭広, 前田金五郎編『岩波古語辞典』東京: 岩波書店.

Ōnuki, Shigeru. *Manyō Shokubutsu Jiten*. Tōkyō: Kureo, 2005. 大貫茂『萬葉植物事典』東京: クレオ.

Shin Nihon Koten Bungaku Taikei, Vol. 6 (Gosen Wakashū). Tōkyō: Iwanami Shoten, 1990. 『新日本古典文学大系 6 （後撰和歌集）』東京: 岩波書店.

Shin Nihon Koten Bungaku Taikei, Vol. 7 (Shūi Wakashū). Tōkyō: Iwanami Shoten, 1990. 『新日本古典文學大系 7 （拾遺和歌集）』東京: 岩波書店.

Shin Nihon Koten Bungaku Taikei, Vol. 8 (Goshūi Wakashū). Tōkyō: Iwanami Shoten, 1994. 『新日本古典文學大系 8 （後拾遺和歌集）』東京: 岩波書店.

Shin Nihon Koten Bungaku Taikei, Vol. 9 (Kin'yō Wakashū, Shika Wakashū). Tōkyō: Iwanami Shoten, 1989. 『新日本古典文學大系 9 （金葉和歌集, 詞花和歌集）』東京: 岩波書店.

Shin Nihon Koten Bungaku Taikei, Vol. 10 (Senzai Wakashū). Tōkyō: Iwanami Shoten, 1993. 『新日本古典文学全集 10 （千載和歌集）』東京：岩波書店.

Shin Nihon Koten Bungaku Taikei, Vol. 19-23 (Genji Monogatari). Tōkyō: Iwanami Shoten, 1993–1997. 『新日本古典文學大系 19-23 （源氏物語）』東京: 岩波書店.

Shin Nihon Koten Bungaku Taikei, Vol. 24 (Tosa Nikki, Kagerō Nikki, Murasaki Shikibu Nikki, Sarashina Nikki). Tōkyō: Iwanami Shoten, 1989. 『新日本古典文學大系 24 （土佐日記, 蜻蛉日記, 紫式部日記, 更級日記）』東京: 岩波書店.

Shin Nihon Koten Bungaku Taikei, Vol. 39 (Hōjōki [includes *Chiteiki*], *Tsurezuregusa*). Tōkyō: Iwanami Shoten, 1989. 『新日本古典文學大系 39 (方丈記 [池亭記 を含む], 徒然草)』東京: 岩波書店.

Shinchō Nihon Koten Shūsei, Vol. 44 (Kinkai Wakashū). Tōkyō: Shinchōsha, 1981. 『新潮 日本古典集成 44 (金塊和歌集)』東京: 新潮社.

Shinchō Nihon Koten Shūsei, Vol. 49 (Sankashū). Tōkyō: Shinchōsha, 1982. 『新潮日本 古典集成 49 (山家集)』東京: 新潮社.

Tanaka, Kimiharu, ed. *Tsurayuki Shū Zenshaku*. Tōkyō: Kazama Shobō, 1997. 田中喜美 春編『貫之集全釈』東京: 風間書房.

Teien Gaku Kōza Vol. 15, Genji Monogatari to Teien. Kyōto: Kyoto University of Art and Design, 2008. 庭園学講座『源氏物語と庭園』第15号. 京都: 京都造形芸術 大学.

Uehara, Keiji, ed. *Kaisetsu Sansui Narabini Yakeizu, Sakuteiki, Vol. 6, Zōen Kosho Sōsho*. Tōkyō: Kashima Shoten, 1972. 上原敬二編『解説　山水並に野形図・作庭 記』造園古書叢書 6. 東京: 加島書店.

Uehara, Keiji. *Zōen Daijiten*. Tōkyō: Kashima Shoten, 1978. 上原敬二『造園大辞典』 東京: 加島書店.

24050990R00139

Made in the USA
Lexington, KY
03 July 2013